Motivate and Reward

Motivate and Reward

Performance Appraisal and Incentive

Systems for Business Success

Herwig W. Kressler

Translated by Simon Pearce

palgrave
macmillan

First published 2003 by
PALGRAVE MACMILLAN
Houndmills, Basingstoke, Hampshire RG21 6XS and
175 Fifth Avenue, New York, N.Y. 10010
Companies and representatives throughout the world

PALGRAVE MACMILLAN is the global academic imprint of the
Palgrave Macmillan division of St. Martin's Press, LLC and of
Palgrave Macmillan Ltd. Macmillan® is a registered trademark in the
United States, United Kingdom and other countries. Palgrave is a
registered trademark in the European Union and other countries.

ISBN 1–4039–0378–6 hardback

This book is printed on paper suitable for recycling and
made from fully managed and sustained forest sources.

A catalogue record for this book is available from the British Library.

Library of Congress Cataloging-in-Publication Data

Kressler, Herwig.
  [Leistungsbeurteilung und Anreizsysteme. English]
  Motivate and reward / Herwig Kressler; translated by Simon Pearce.
    p. cm.
Includes bibliographical references and index.
  1. Employee motivation. 2. Performance--Evaluation. 3. Incentive
awards. I. Title.
  HF5549.5.M63 K74 2003
  658.3'14--dc21

                                        2002193096

Editing and origination by Curran Publishing Services, Norwich

10 9 8 7 6 5 4 3 2 1
12 11 10 09 08 07 06 05 04 03

Printed and bound in Great Britain by
Creative Print & Design (Wales), Ebbw Vale

CONTENTS

Contents

LIST OF FIGURES

Motivation, performance capacity, development potential: these are the most essential factors when undertaking and fulfilling any task. Successfully accomplishing a task in any conceivable organization – be it an economic enterprise, a non-profit-making or charitable organization, an association, cooperation or political party – depends ultimately upon these three elements. It is first and foremost through them that skills, experiences, talents, latent abilities and creative energies are activated. They also play a decisive role in achieving the goals by which an organization measures its success and justifies its existence.

I spent many years working in a teaching capacity and in leading positions with international personnel-policy responsibilities. During this time it became clear to me how important it is to understand what motivates people in particular ways and to particular ends, to understand how to achieve high levels of performance that assure one company more success than another. Why do some people stride through their careers, gaining along the way a high degree of responsibility and influence, establishing companies, leading them to success, reforming them and always seeming able to nurture the necessary resourcefulness to maintain that success, whereas others do not seem able to do this, or do not want to, or simply never attempt it?

Wherever we look we can observe huge differences in what is commonly called motivation, in performance levels and in development potential. Understanding the essence of motivation, performance, potential and reward is complicated by a confusing variety of definitions. These are invariably put forward and scrutinized so that the factors that determine success may be grasped as thoroughly and quickly as possible to give the edge over competitors. Not everything, however, can be found in the Aladdin's cave of explanations and definitions.

Definitions can become hackneyed or vague, and acquire new meanings through such widespread and varied use. One of the victims of this is 'motivation'. It is commonly believed that people can be motivated by pay. Pay, reward and incentive are all types of benefits, types of stimuli that can be employed as a means for differentiating between tasks, functions, performance, success and results. All sorts of things, some extremely positive, may be achieved in this way. But this will not achieve sustained *motivation*. Motivation and incentive are often used synonymously, but this obscures both terms: motivation is underestimated and the demands on incentives are placed too high.

What someone can achieve today in one capacity is often mistaken for what that person can achieve tomorrow in another, more responsible capacity, often with disastrous consequences for the company and the people involved. Failed careers are less often due to lack of ability and talent than to miscalculation of future potential.

In order to avoid a great deal of confusion and ambiguity I have endeavoured to examine these terms thoroughly, to explain and demonstrate which factors can be employed to the advantage of people and organizations. I will draw particular attention to the dangers of misleading interpretations or of misuse of the terms.

It will be necessary to use certain technical terms, but these will be explained and demonstrated as practically as possible. The guiding principle will be simplicity. When a particular system or process can be demonstrated satisfactorily with three illustrations of its components, then for speed, ease and efficiency this will be done, rather than adding five further examples out of a desire for perfection. The law of diminishing returns applies without exception.

Systems and technical terms should be explained as simply as possible and only embellished where absolutely necessary.

On the other hand, one should not be too succinct when it comes to understanding. It is worth learning as much as there is to know about motivation. If a 'motivation-system' existed, then I would follow the guiding principle: as simply as possible. Because motivation concerns understanding, however, the following principle applies: be as comprehensive as possible. At this point it is useful to look back on and learn from the ideas and research of others. In the section on motivation, therefore, I will review briefly the most important theories and ideas of what motivates people to work; that may help readers to form their own opinions and tailor-made concepts. It was, after all, no less than Isaac Newton who said that if he could see further than others then it was because he stood on the shoulders of giants. We should not take it for granted that everything new is also good. When it comes to knowledge we need to separate the wheat from the chaff, even with theories that are years or even decades old. Theories that are still valid today have already withstood considerable scrutiny. Thus it is that 'everything you ever wanted to know about motivation, but were too scared to ask' is a much longer – and perhaps for some more exciting – chapter than 'everything about share options'.

In two earlier books published in German in 1989 and 1993, I wrote extensively about matters such as performance evaluation, assessment of potential, management development, pay, organization structure and culture. When my Austrian publishers suggested I should approach evaluation, performance incentives and everything to do with this subject in a new way, I embraced the idea wholeheartedly. It gave me the opportunity to give a broad view of developments, to create a synthesis from experience, and to establish a link between the elements that might make the difference between success and failure, between average and exceptional results.

The following study examines the relevant issues in three main sections.

- The first discusses motivation. Here general aspects lead to specific points on motivation to work. The most important theories and hypotheses are described and commented upon. Leading principles dealing with motivation are outlined. Finally, the most important difference between motivation and incentive is illustrated.
- The second major section deals with the evaluation of performance and potential. It will examine the relevance of evaluation, the meaning and purpose of performance evaluations in organizations, and the influence of structure, culture, and leadership style. Questions of how performance evaluations are perceived, as well as their varied characteristics and methods, will be discussed.

    The evaluation of potential, which, significant as it is, is so often misunderstood, will be dealt with in depth. The driving force behind potential will be scrutinized in detail, as well as a whole host of criteria that have been empirically researched and actually employed in evaluations of potential.
- The third main section deals with reward strategies, payment systems, incentive or stimulus systems, and financial participation, with specific focus on share options. The examination of reward strategies will also embrace principles and objectives, and further discuss the possibilities and limitations of their employment in practise.

The list of contents is extremely detailed in order to facilitate the search for a particular subject. The individual chapters are thematically linked, but are structured so that they may be read as separate units without losing any meaning.

I am grateful to Stephen Rutt of Palgrave Macmillan for his interest in my work and for the support I received from him and his colleagues in preparing the English language edition of this book. I very much appreciate Simon Pearce's efforts in translating the German original into English.

Herwig W. Kressler
Vienna, 2002

PART I

Motivation

Motives – Desires – Motivational Factors

Nothing happens without a reason; everything has a cause. There are both good and bad reasons just as there are clear and unclear causes. Expectation, hope, fear, obligation, reward, ambition, helpfulness, determination, the need for admiration, habit, ritual, need and countless other factors, whether real or imagined, influence our behaviour, actions and reactions, our common lives and experiences, and not least our world of work.

Everybody has motives, is 'motivated'. The term 'motivated' should, however, be understood in its proper sense. In common parlance 'to be motivated' is above all a positive condition, something desirable that should be promoted by a whole host of agents, or 'motivational factors', in order to encourage the desire to enhance performance. Understood in this way, however, 'motivation' is at best useful shorthand in business language, but this concept is too weak to provide a proper understanding.

When we say that everybody always has motives, is therefore continuously 'motivated', this is of course not to say that everybody feels constantly spurred on to higher and the highest levels of performance. One may be motivated either to do something or not to do something; to strive for something or avoid something; to win somebody over, to convince, to persuade; to achieve success or avoid failure; to become famous or remain inconspicuous; to lead or be led; to attack or search for safety; to plan for the future or live each day as it comes … in short, everything we do, or do not do, has its own motive.

'Motive' means literally the mainspring, the impetus, the rationale behind any action. (It can also mean the distinctive idea of a work of art, but this meaning is not relevant to our study.) The term has been common coinage since the sixteenth century and, according to the 1963 *Duden Etymology*, derives from the Medieval Latin word 'motivum'.

Each instance of our behaviour, action and even inaction has its own cause, impetus and motive. It is not surprising therefore that the formation, development and shaping of these stimuli play a vital part, one could without exaggeration say an all-embracing part, in our lives. Even in day-to-day social life within families and other groups a range of motives arise again and again, leading to the broadest possible variety of behaviour and action. The same thing happens, albeit at a very different intensity and with a varying degree of influence, in school and in education in general, through religious and philosophical perspectives and convictions. All forms of cultural expression, art, literature and music underpin reasons, motives and ideas. The many forms of the media and their means of communication may not always be seen as manifestations of culture, but they are nevertheless a crucial part of our civilization and constantly emit signals that influence opinion and behaviour. In attempting to outdo their rivals in the war for a share of the market, producers and salesmen advertise with the widest variety of methods. In this way many people become both the agent and the object of advertising campaigns.

> In the end everybody who works in businesses and other organizations is subject to certain influences that affect behaviour. This need not even have anything to do with targeted 'motivational measures'. More everyday means can generate aspirations in the workers, giving them impetus and activating motives: having a specific task, being responsible for something, having a part to play, having goals to work towards, achieving a certain level of performance and knowing what is expected of them.

Most people in businesses are 'employees'. This is relevant not so much in the formal sense of industrial law as in the context of motivation. It is manifest above all in group membership, belonging to a team, the identification (or lack of identification) with business objectives. It also refers to how the employee sees the quality and value of the business or the institution in terms of its product, service, contribution to the quality of social life and the manner in which conflict situations are resolved. This can mean a business's philosophy towards conflict resolution: whether problems are discussed openly and conflicts approached objectively without emotion, or whether internal lobbying, behind-the-scenes diplomacy and perhaps even intrigue are more the norm.

Moreover, the manner in which a business resolves conflicts in its external relations will shape an employee's desires, stimuli and way of thinking, thus generating motives for certain behaviour and action. We should also take into consideration the fact that, quite apart from the aforementioned social and cultural relationships and affiliations, almost everybody also belongs to more or less informal groups, including circles of friends, clubs and all sorts of associations. It can thus be seen that an intricate and complex web of influences, rules, value systems, loyalties and interactions, all of which affect the motive for individual action, is unfolding.

Motivation to Work

Ever since it was discovered that employee performance held the key to business success, there have been continuous efforts to understand the various desires that help to optimize the intensity, quality, efficiency and reliability of performance. It is just as necessary for employees to be motivated as it is for them to be qualified. Although human work has existed in one form or another ever since people have walked the planet, the motivation to work has only very recently been the subject of study (only since the 1920s).

Before this time, insofar as there was any formal incorporation into, for example, the industrial organization and processes of work, people were so much a part of the running of a business that the question of motive was easily answered: everybody had his or her 'place'. Each person was a smaller or larger cog in the greater machinery, grinding away at predominantly physical labour.

This inescapable system was reinforced by the fact that work was essential as a source of income, as the basis of existence in a world that lacked a social safety net. Moreover, the Christian world at least viewed work as fundamental (it was, after all, Adam who was sentenced to eat his bread in the sweat of his brow) and it also constituted the ethical and moral cornerstone of social order. In strictly economic terms one could classify the need to work as a 'factor of production' alongside the need for capital and land. Political teaching and ideology, economic and business management theories, and the practice of management itself all took account of this notion.

The vast majority of human history lies in pre-industrial times, and even after the Industrial Revolution a large part of the population continued to operate in non-industrial structures such as agriculture and the countless number of small crafts. In these structures people were so integrated in day-to-day events that, rather than being subordinate to unavoidable processes, they largely determined these processes themselves. Nothing could happen without the farmers and their wives, their children, the milkmaids and the stableboys. It is difficult to ascertain whether the motivation to work was an issue. The driving force behind work seems partly to have been necessity: there was little else that people could turn their hands to. It also arose out of an unquestioned logic that closely balanced not only input with yield, but also, on the one hand, direct accountability and clearly perceived individual responsibility with, on the other hand, the correspondingly inescapable dependence of the workforce. It is uncertain which proved the more effective means of motivation: the necessity to work or the unquestioned logic of working in harmony with both natural and market forces, which emerged partly from supporting individual needs and partly from trading and exchanging in the more or less immediate neighbourhood. The answer is most likely a combination of the two, and this remains the case where structures remain traditionally based on agriculture and craftsmanship.

Motivation and Frustration

The question of what motivation actually is cannot be answered merely by stating that it arises out of life's material necessities. That would be too simplistic and misleading. If it were indeed the case, then it would follow that once these requirements had been fulfilled a situation would result in which motivation did not exist or did not play a part. It is generally accepted, however, that this is not the case, and we do not have to delve too deeply to prove this. In the main there is no lack of motivation even among people with very high incomes, people whose wealth is so great that they could certainly live off it for the rest of their lives without the slightest risk to their basic requirements. Indeed, most such people are constantly spurred on to further pursuits. (Of course there are some who display more passive tendencies, although this too is a form of motivation inasmuch as they strive to do as little as possible; these people, however, are common in all income brackets.) If the assumption were true that motivation, in the sense of an impetus to act, depended on how well basic life requirements were supplied, then it would certainly follow that once they were met the intensity of activity would decrease, and vice versa. Since this is clearly not the case it may be asserted that as basic needs are fulfilled new requirements continuously take their place, ensuring that motivational levels are constantly renewed. This is in many respects a positive process, yet it also has certain limitations. These limitations are even more dramatically reinforced if the requirements refer only to material necessities, rather than also including immaterial, intellectual and spiritual goals and considerations. Our needs embrace a very broad scope, which is certainly far more complex and difficult to define – and even more difficult to measure – than the exclusively material scope outlined above.

Furthermore, particular needs will not generate the same degree of motivation in all circumstances. The influence they have does not simply correlate with the strength of the need, but is affected by how likely it is that the need in question can indeed be satisfactorily fulfilled. When something is a lost cause, or even seen to be a lost cause, the brakes will be put on the motivational drive. Indeed, there is even a change of direction as the motivation to achieve a goal gives way to its opposite: namely, to put a stop to every effort, forget about that particular aim, and avoid 'throwing good money after bad'.

We see here what is in effect the opposite pole to motivation, namely 'frustration'. 'Frusta' is the Latin word for 'in vain'. Something is not, or ceases to be, a matter of concern because it is 'in vain', because the effort would lead to nothing, because there can be no (or no measurable) achievement.

> In truth frustration is not the antithesis to motivation. Rather it is posited on the negative end of the motivation spectrum, where the watchword is 'leave it alone, it makes no sense, do not trouble yourself'. Frustration is therefore also a form of motivation, albeit one that promotes inaction, avoidance and refusal.

It is in no way purely theoretical rhetoric to place motivation and frustration on one and the same continuum. On the contrary, seeing motivation not as a fixed term with one single value, but as multifaceted, actually facilitates understanding. Motivation is not only multifaceted in the sense that frustration occupies one end of the spectrum while at the other extreme is what we might call 'hypermotivation' (an extreme form of motivation where the driving force is so powerful that it leads to a type of hyperactivity). There is more to it than simply those who are motivated and those who are frustrated. Quite apart from the various shades in between, there are also those who overdo it, who work day and night, for whom no result is ever good enough, who want to surpass all objectives, for whom no effort is ever too much, who are driven on to achieve something more or to attain even greater perfection. Unlike those deterred by frustration, not only are they undaunted by major obstacles, but they also disregard the fact that what they might actually achieve may not correspond at all to what they set out to gain. The law of diminishing return means nothing to them.

Motivation is Highly Personal

Motivation is not only relative, it also depends heavily on individual circum-stances. If a number of people were exposed to identical conditions, they would assume very different positions on a motivation scale. (This is not to suggest that an absolute 'motivation scale' exists or is even desirable.)

> Different people react in extremely varied ways to 'motivational factors' or even environmental influences. Some tend towards frustration, avoidance, refusal and submission, while others become highly motivated when they are confronted by a particular challenge. We may speak of a 'frustration threshold', which can vary dramatically from person to person.

This is often observable in the ways different people react to identical goals. A particular goal (making a sale, making profit, cost saving etc.) may be rejected by one person as too high, by another as too low, even if both of them are quite capable of achieving it. The sort of person who would reject the goal as being too high would probably view *going beyond* the goal as 'motivating'; this would explain the desire for a yardstick that could be surpassed. The person who rejects it as too low, however, measures himself or herself *against the difficulty* of the goal, and this explains the preference for a higher target that is the limit of what the person can achieve. It is clear then that attitudes towards any given task are fundamentally influenced by the various ways in which someone might be motivated.

If Person A's response to a target of 100 is to suggest that 90 would be far more realistic, and to support this with a range of rational arguments, then that does not necessarily indicate inadequate eagerness, lack of spirit or excessive caution. On the contrary, it might even show a rather more subtly effective motive: to shine by exceeding expectations. This person may not really anticipate any difficulty in fulfilling the target of 100, but ultimately wants to guarantee that reaching it means more than just achieving a set goal. So that Person A's own expectations can be met, the achievement of 100 should be juxtaposed against a set objective of 90 or 95. This would accom-modate that person's specific needs and provide an effective motive.

So many time-consuming, irritating and, in the true sense of the word, 'frustrating' discussions about target setting could be avoided – or at least shortened and brought to a satisfactory conclusion – if the contracting parties could acknowledge, either explicitly or tacitly, the motives that give rise to apparent differences of opinion.

Thus by recommending that the targets be reduced, Person A is not saying 'give me a goal that I can achieve more easily', but 'I need a goal that I can surpass so that I feel satisfied with myself'. In the final analysis Person A desires any achievement to be recognized as a 'brilliant triumph'.

It is not entirely unrealistic of Person B, on the other hand, to maintain that 100 is a goal that does not exactly demand high ambition. This is someone who wants to be challenged, yearns to be entrusted with much more, perhaps even ventures to propose that more could be achieved than had previously been supposed. Person B does not imply 'you are making a mistake, I know better', but 'to make the task attractive to me I need to be challenged beyond what is normally expected'. Person B is therefore not 'frustrated' if this higher goal is not achieved; in actual fact s/he never really thought that it could be. Such people desire, however, that their self-image in 'heroic struggles' be maintained.

> In practice objectives are frequently lumped together so that there is little scope for focusing on individually specific motives. This standardization is often underscored by bland incentive or bonus systems, often to the detriment of motivation.

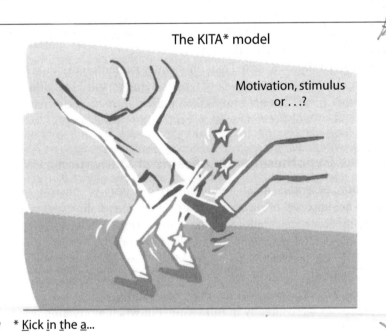

The KITA* model

Motivation, stimulus or . . .?

* Kick in the a...

If 100 is a 'difficult' target for A and an 'easy' one for B, then it is actually unsuitable for both. If it is apparent that fulfilling this standardized goal will achieve an equally standardized bonus of 10, then both A and B will look sceptically upon how their performance relates to their pay.

The availability, however, of an extra payment – varying according to the degree to which the objective is fulfilled – opens up another dimension. The original responses, made up of personal notions that the objective was 'too difficult' or 'too easy', are now superseded by an extremely powerful stimulus: striving either to obtain the bonus or to preclude the possibility of not obtaining it. In these circumstances the target is almost always criticized by the potential bonus recipient as being unrealistically high and hardly ever as too undemanding.

This cannot always be explained in terms of superficial opportunism and greed. The most conclusive evidence that any particular activity has been successful is when it is specifically and clearly rewarded within the framework of an incentive or bonus system. It is more straightforward therefore to work towards this easily recognizable form of acknowledgement, rather than to lay stress on decidedly more delicate and individually determined notions of performance and success. This also explains why many bonus systems that are 'dependent upon success' do not in the long term lead to payment which is felt to be fair and justified – neither do they lead to a perceptibly higher degree of motivation. (That is in no way to suggest that forms of pay based on performance and success are necessarily inefficient!)

It can generally be asserted that uniformity neglects individual shades of motive and thereby runs the risk of targets being missed. Individualization, on the other hand, can help to awaken potential, raise performance levels and generate a workforce that takes pride in its successes.

Theories, Hypotheses and Concepts of Motivation to Work

Motivation embraces many fields and is not only of interest to behaviourists but also of prime concern in the world of business and work. Hence, in order to supplement the observations made so far, we will endeavour to set out various theories and hypotheses on motivation, and specifically on motivation to work. Motivation has only been acknowledged relatively recently as a differentiating factor in performance. Therefore this overview will begin by considering the period when industrial processes were already in full swing, but when motivation was still an alien concept.

'Scientific Management'

During the emergence of industrial mass production it was the insights of so-called 'scientific management' that established more order in and raised the efficiency of increasingly extensive manufacturing and administrative business processes. It was a time of meticulous time-and-motion studies, of production lines, of offices with hundreds of typewriters, of accounts departments with hundreds of files, with the staff operating as an integral part of the precise time-and-motion routine of well-rehearsed processes. The staff was just as much a tool to be utilized as were all the other machines of business. Motivation was not even an issue. On the contrary, conformity and subordination were more in demand than individuality or creativity, at least as far as the great number of workers and the large majority of the office personnel were concerned.

Frederick Winslow Taylor, who, as one of the leading lights in this school of management, gave his name to 'Taylorism', made a very typical statement: 'Now one of the first requirements for a man who is fit to handle pig iron is that he shall be so stupid and phlegmatic that he more nearly resembles the ox than any other type.' It is said that Henry Ford ordered his employees to hang up not only their coats in the cloakroom when they came to work, but also their souls.

Both of these comments were meant in all seriousness and illustrate the position and status that people had as part of standardized, regulated and predetermined processes. These people could not have any influence upon such processes, for this would have only caused disruption.

Trust in Technology and Utilitarianism

There was a complete absence of even the slightest trace of acknowledging human needs, respecting individual values or encouraging talent and potential. This absence has its roots in an era and a cultural climate that viewed the working world in two crucially important ways.

First, there was an almost unconditional trust in technology. This is not surprising considering the dramatic rise in productivity that technological advances had enabled. Almost everything that human power alone could hitherto achieve was suddenly eclipsed to an astonishing degree by better and faster machines. In the new factories, people became the weak link in the chain. They were still indispensable, but had to conform and be subordinate to new regimes. If this proved impossible, then people became a dangerous risk factor, potentially jeopardizing the high returns promised by extremely capital-intensive technological equipment. Technology and its further advance, therefore, were to be encouraged wherever scope allowed, while at the same time people had to adapt as much as possible to this dominating force. This meant that, compared with today, factories in the first half of the twentieth century had a high staffing level. At that time, even in places where production lines were already in place, hundreds or even thousands of people were needed to carry out the necessary chores and activities to run the production process as quickly, efficiently and faultlessly as possible. It was still, after all, light-years away from robots and electronic steering devices. People had to perform these roles as much like machines and as little like humans as possible.

The second crucial factor was a high degree of utilitarianism: this both complied with and extended the belief in technology. A very fundamental belief in utility viewed the working relationship as primarily a reciprocal exchange of service, in which both of the contracting parties, that is the employer and employee, were entitled to put their own interests first. Emotional bonds, mutual loyalty or dependence, patriarchal relationships and paternalistic lord and servant allegiances were alien to this functional model, which hinged more on necessity and utility than courtesy and emotion.

This utilitarianism suited above all the cultural, historical and religious background of North America and – if to a slightly less extent – of Northwest Europe. In the rest of Europe and even more in South America, Africa and Asia, the pace of industrialization was not only completely different, but also the social and cultural emphasis was less material and more spiritual. Western utilitarianism found here, if at all, only a limited foothold. We can imagine the different interactions that might take place between industrial or economic development and either predominantly material or more strongly spiritual world views, especially considering the various driving forces or motives that arise from these so completely different basic positions.

It is, however, true that economic industrialization makes rapid progress in those countries where a close connection between technological advance and fundamental utilitarianism in delivering performance makes it possible to subordinate humans to technology. This is in contrast to countries where the working relationship has other, less material and more emotional aspects, which are often valued above pure necessity or utility. It should not be forgotten that industrial progress depends on other factors too. These include access to the markets, the availability of roads and transport, the mobility of the workforce, capital and the readiness to take risks. It is, however, all too often forgotten that for all sorts of reasons people can exercise a strong, often determining influence on success, growth and development. This was apparent at the time of 'scientific management', only it was more narrowly defined. In the case of most blue and white-collar workers it was defined in terms of producing work to exact specifications, and being paid for this in ways that were just as precise; anything else would have been superfluous decoration.

> In today's working world such an attitude would not only be ethically and morally indefensible, it would also be wholly counterproductive econom- ically. What is needed today is the ability to work as an individual and as a team member with high creativity, initiative, responsibility, applying and developing talents, continuing to learn and being willing to offer and adapt to innovation. Motivation and performance are thus decisive vari- ables that can determine success. Where once technology had almost mythical, belief-inspiring status, technological advance has become quite normal; and a reciprocal pattern of service in return for service, in both a material and an immaterial sense, has taken the place of utilitarianism.

Even today it might be said there is sufficient reason for a resurgent belief in technology, due to what seems an often unconditional trust in informa- tion technology, or even a new utilitarianism, arising out of remorselessly increasing competitive pressure. The importance of motivation and of the capacity and willingness to perform, however, is today so widely recog- nized that cost factors now take a clear second place to the far more sig- nificant competitive advantage that can be gained by factoring in desires, motives and motivation.

It is necessary here, however, to return in our observations to the starting- point, for we have yet to provide a satisfactory formulation of a concept explaining the motivation to work.

The 'Discovery' of the Motivation to Work

In the 1920s a groundbreaking discovery was made which changed forev- er the way a person's role in the industrial working world was viewed. It was based on the results of a study that would later gain acclaim as the 'Hawthorne Experiment'. It was certainly not the only force behind a change in thinking, but it is the most well known.

The Hawthorne Experiment was named after the Hawthorne factory of the US Western Electric Company in Cicero, Illinois. In this factory a study was carried out according to the principles of scientific manage- ment and cost optimization. Its purpose was to examine how peripheral working conditions could influence the quantity and quality of worker

output. Part of the study assessed whether, if conditions were reduced below a certain level, the fall in quality of output would outweigh any savings in costs. To this end the lighting was gradually dimmed in certain sections of the factory and at selected work stations. In other parts of the factory no changes were made. Productivity was then measured in terms of both quantity and quality. Workers were also observed during the course of this lengthy study in order to ascertain the stage at which signs of tiredness became visible.

What was most surprising about the results of the study was that they proved exactly the opposite of what was expected: in no way did the workers' performance worsen as the working conditions measurably and verifiably deteriorated. The opposite happened: it improved! Performance remained constant in the sections of the factory where no alterations were made; indeed it even declined over time. Perhaps it is unnecessary to say that the workers were not informed about the methods and objectives of the study; it was almost unknown at that time to inform employees about plans and changes. In more concrete terms it was feared that if workers knew about the changes in working conditions, which were invariably changes for the worse, then in their own interests they would influence the results of the study by intentionally reducing their performance.

One can perhaps imagine the researchers scratching their heads as they examined the completely unexpected effects of their measures. This inexplicable result was replicated time and again, however, so a theory had to be found that could explain this hitherto unknown correlation between a mysterious cause and its verified effect. An explanation was finally found: The Hawthorne workers were used to carrying out their work according to a set routine. There were never any irregularities, everything ran like clockwork. But now, because this study of the influence of peripheral working conditions was being undertaken, certain groups and work stations were suddenly placed under observation, while others were as usual not monitored. The 'guinea-pigs', who did not know what the activity was all about, felt suddenly elevated: they had the feeling that they must be doing something special to deserve so much attention. On the one hand then, there was a positive feeling of acknowledgement, but they also felt somewhat threatened as their work was being brought into question. The result was that not only were the effects of the tangible deterioration of working conditions balanced out by the workers' enhanced performance, but were even overcompensated by it.

A new dimension began to unfold: the human as a subject with potential. There were clearly more effective means of realizing and developing this potential in the working world than mere subordination to the processes of production. Human Relations became a new consideration that might also be of serious economic value.

So a new factor, which over time would gain increasing significance, was added to the primacy of technology and the principle of utilitarianism.

Further Developments

Consequently there was a growing interest in both empirical and theoretical studies into the cause and essence of the motivation to work, as well into the various ways in which motivation functions.

We are not likely to find one satisfactory and all-embracing definition of the motivation to work. Aspects of each theory and hypothesis can be disputed. On the other hand, if one wishes to develop and apply a personal concept for a business, office relationships or even a manner of leadership, it can only be beneficial to reflect upon the essence and principles of motivation.

As already indicated, motivation is a highly personal affair. As such it does not depend on the confirmation or rejection of particular theories.

What is peculiar to the diverse theories and hypotheses of motivation is the systematic examination of a phenomenon that is otherwise rather difficult to define. Becoming familiar with some of these definitions or attempts at definition has the advantage of creating a contemplative backdrop, from which the motivation phenomenon and thereby an analysis of personal motivation behaviour is more easily accessible. Furthermore, on this basis the effect that personal behaviour might have on the motivation of others can be better understood.

Definitions of motivation derive from highly personal thought processes and privately formed concepts of the phenomenon. Perhaps that may sound a little esoteric, but it is not. As with so many aspects of leadership and the working world, motivation concerns a fundamental human trait. This applies in part to target setting, judging people, assessing situations, deciding courses of action, planning for the future, estimating risks, communicating, criticizing and having 'aspirations'. These and many other activities and thought processes are by nature peculiar to humans. These abilities evolve through development, learning and experience, some to a greater extent than others, depending on whether they prove more or less 'successful' or 'worthwhile'. Thus throughout the course of our lives we become more 'competent' in these matters.

This natural trait of motivation, specifically the motivation to work, is of significance in the working world, as we spend part of our lives as employees in a business, members of an institution or representatives of a team. It is helpful therefore to become familiar with ideas and concepts so that the processes that take place within us and in our relationships with others are clearer. This clarification leads to understanding and that in turn facilitates a more informed choice of decisions and behaviour, which can positively influence both our own state of motivation and that of others. This influence is in no way restricted to hierarchical structures or laws. Its presence can be felt wherever scope for action, lines of communication and areas of responsibility meet or overlap. Every member of an organization who interacts with another exercises – positively or negatively – a motivating influence. This influence may be strong or weak, but it is always present. The same applies to interactions among members of external organizations, such as customers, suppliers, authorities, competitors or associations.

Motivation Theories: an Overview

In order to understand better the various terms and forms of the motivation to work, it is useful to review some theories and hypotheses that extensive expert research has provided.

It is desirable here – just as it is elsewhere – to avoid the tempting but misleading concept of 'motivation techniques', and neither would we advocate a new belief in technology. Theories, hypotheses and speculations aim to explain or define matters that are uncertain. They do not prescribe, but offer food for thought. We occasionally hear mention of techniques and methods of motivation or see them in action, but they are mostly geared to the disposition and nature of the person employing them, and how they are employed is the result of highly individual consideration. Thus motivation techniques do not travel well, and what might be a method for one is a means of manipulation for another. There is no such thing as an off-the-peg motivation technique that can be employed with the same chances of success as an overhead projector or a new piece of software.

In view of the need to formulate a personal concept of work motivation, it is advisable to refer to some of the fundamental arguments that earlier thinkers have very zealously tried and tested.

Maslow

One of the first comprehensive theories about motivation, which discussed primarily the motivation to work, was mapped out by Abraham H. Maslow (*A Theory of Human Motivation*, 1943). Maslow was not the first to try to explain human motivation; Sigmund Freud, Carl Jung and others did a great deal of interesting work. But Maslow developed the concept of the 'Pyramid of Requirements' or 'Hierarchy of Needs', which proved to give a very revealing view of the subject and lent itself well to the working world.

By applying both abstract philosophical deliberation and clinical observation Maslow was able to identify five categories of human needs. Each of these needs is posited at a particular level. In this scheme of a pyramid or hierarchy, higher level needs are addressed only when those on the immediately lower level have been satisfied. Maslow's conclusion is particularly relevant to motivation behaviour. He argues that needs that are not (fully) satisfied have a 'motivating' effect, giving the impetus for certain behaviour or action that should bring about the satisfaction of the need. This, however, only functions when all of the needs on the lower level have been met. In this way, therefore, only unsatisfied needs are 'motivators'. According to Maslow it is possible to meet all but those needs posited on the highest level (five): these are of a type for which there is no closure.

The individual needs are as follows:

Level 5: The Need for Self-Actualization
Understanding the world; acquiring wisdom; clarifying life's objectives; achieving independence; developing creativity and individuality.

Level 4: Esteem Needs
Being acknowledged and esteemed by others; gaining self-confidence; having success; attaining knowledge, power, prestige, status and dignity.

Level 3: Love Needs (Affection and Belonging)
Looking for love and affection; belonging (to a family, a circle of friends, a group, a union, a business); attaining social security; avoiding loneliness, rejection and rootlessness.

Level 2: Security Needs
Need for physical security, including security in a figurative sense: stability, reliability, freedom from fear, threat and chaos; avoiding uncertainty; protection through law and order.

Level 1: Physiological Needs

Nourishment, clothing and accommodation; sexuality; rest and relaxation, but also a need for activity and movement.

Maslow's concept of various levels of needs is tempting with its clarity and logic. It is with good reason that it is still one of the most quoted and consulted analyses of motivation, both in theoretical and practical examinations of the theme. Maslow's theory is, of course, not undisputed; almost every theory in every field will have its opponents. Obviously his concept cannot be applied universally, infallibly and without exception to everyone. What it does give, however, is a series of explanations of human behaviour and also an account of why identical measures may not always generate the same drive towards fulfilling objectives.

Lower level needs must be met before higher level ones. When (perhaps in an economic depression) wages are so low that primary needs can hardly be met, it makes little sense to spend money on employee information, celebrating anniversaries or holding company parties. All viable expenditure should then flow into income. On the other hand, when physiological and security needs are satisfied, then employee information can play a very positive and motivating role in the generation of community spirit (level 3). Like any other rule, this may not apply to everybody. There are people who would prefer to cut down spending on food and clothing if instead they could go to the theatre. This, however, is the exception rather than the

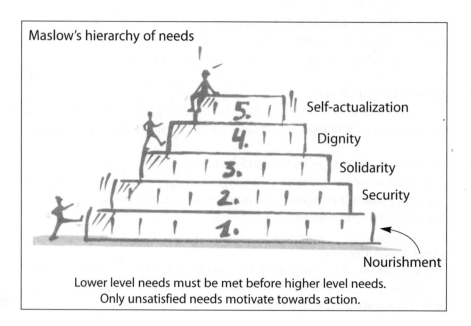

Maslow's hierarchy of needs

5. Self-actualization
4. Dignity
3. Solidarity
2. Security
1. Nourishment

Lower level needs must be met before higher level needs.
Only unsatisfied needs motivate towards action.

rule. 'Food comes first, then morals' Bertolt Brecht announced to the world, a position Maslow would naturally endorse.

McGregor

While Maslow deals with a general theory of human motivation that can also be applied to the motivation to work, Douglas McGregor (*The Human Side of Enterprise*, 1957) deals specifically with the behaviour of people within an organization, a business or a company. To this end McGregor formulated his 'Theory X' and 'Theory Y'.

According to Theory X, work is unpleasant for the average person in the modern world. People feel an almost innate reluctance to work and try to avoid it wherever possible. It is therefore necessary to bear down on people in a work situation, to put them under pressure and to threaten them with punishments. Only in this way can business objectives be met. If work were left to those who volunteered for it or even enjoyed it, then everything would grind to a halt. Moreover, people not only normally try to avoid work, but also prefer to be led and guided, shunning responsibility and desiring security above all.

Theory Y stands in contrast to this. Work is physical and mental activity. Hence it is something completely normal, natural and desirable for the average person. Work is as natural a part of human life as leisure or recreation. Being forced to work is therefore not only unnecessary, but detrimental to achieving objectives. Ultimately it is important that work presents a challenge when it is faced, and provides satisfaction when it has been performed.

With his two theories McGregor is in effect portraying two different points of view. These, he suggests, underlie two contrasting, but equally typical types of management behaviour, working relationship and employee motivation. The one type of manager adheres to Theory X, and the other believes in Theory Y. Even if a manager has never heard of either theory, he or she will behave according to one or the other.

If it is accepted not only that management acts according to one of the two theories, but also that employee expectations and work attitudes fall under their umbrella, then both of the two concepts might prove expedient. The values, however, must be correct: an 'X'-Manager and 'X'-Employees will mutually complement one another. Belief in the need for strong authoritative leadership and hierarchical structures will correspond to the expectation of strict regulations and clear areas of responsibility, and this will be beneficial to both parties. The expectations of both management and employee govern how the tasks and the work are to be structured:

McGregor

Superior	Type X	Leadership through order, coercion, control
Employee	Type X	Hates work, must be coerced
Superior	Type Y	Leadership through challenge, recognition, promotion
Employee	Type Y	Loves activity, hankers after challenge and fulfilment

---

objectives might be reached, not reached or perhaps surpassed, but the working behaviour is felt as normal and no alteration deemed necessary. Supporters of Theory X would view this as a confirmation of their roles.

There will be a similar effect when a 'Y'-Manager has 'Y'-employees. The management, having a participative approach and ruling by consensus, will correspond to the expectations of employees: employees will work on their own initiative, the management echelons will be *primus inter pares* and hierarchical status will have little meaning. There will be targets here, too, some achieved, some not. But just as with the example of 'X', management and employee behaviour that accords to a shared belief in theory 'Y' will be rewarded as effective. Supporters of Theory Y will, therefore, have every opportunity to find proof of their code's validity.

Consequently, it can be concluded from the illustration above that one thing should most definitely not happen: that an 'X'-Manager has 'Y'-Employees or vice versa. The symmetry would inevitably be disrupted and there would then be a catastrophic effect on motivation and cooperation.

Stepping outside the abstract planes of Theories X and Y for a moment, it is clear that in reality there are few who belong exclusively to one or the other theory. Thus it is not enough to say 'I am obviously an X-Manager, therefore I am looking only for X-Employees and this is for everyone's benefit'. Even if it were practically possible to appoint such a targeted selection it would be counterproductive, as other selection criteria, such as knowledge, experience and competence should be the main considerations.

It might be valuable, therefore, to find a synthesis of elements of both theories and their opposites. This synthesis should take into account the fact that we all – or at least most of us – have elements of both Theory X and Theory Y in us.

If this is true, then it is to be expected that people exercise self-control and self-discipline in the workplace when they feel committed to meeting certain objectives. Because these objectives to some extent become the employee's own goals, authoritative or punitive intervention should be unnecessary.

The extent of commitment and devotion to the task depends on the rewards that can be expected for achieving the objective or fulfilling the task. If the conditions for it are right, people are thoroughly prepared to take on responsibility instead of shying away from it. Financial payment is part, although not the whole, of compensation or reward. Recognizing performance and success can also be accomplished through praise, positive feedback, offering development possibilities and similar steps. Combining financial and emotional measures always proves most effective.

Most people have talent, power of imagination, creativity and faculty for judgement, all of which are needed to solve the most complex problems. In McGregor's opinion, it is difficult to make use of more than a small part of these talents in the generally prevailing working environment. This certainly colours any picture of an ideal world. Structures, communication, the decision-making processes and frequently also the business culture are often the causes of problems and obstacles. This sounds extremely negative, but it is important to look at this realistically: businesses do not find themselves in an ideal world; the management is not entirely free to make decisions or set priorities; and there are just as often external as well as internal pressures which necessitate trade-offs between what is desired and what is attainable.

The theories and hypotheses of McGregor help, therefore, to give a clear sense of direction with a dose of realism; for although we are still quite a way off from the 'best of all worlds', we can at least reduce the distance.

Argyris

McGregor's premise assumed an almost 'pre-programmed' contrast between the function of an organization and the expectations and potential of the people within it. Similarly, Chris Argyris (*Personality and Organization*, 1957) emphasizes the gap between human potential and the conditions that can generally be found in the working world. Argyris finds that in most organizations and industrial structures, including businesses, there are insufficient opportunities for people to fulfil their need for self-actualization (see Maslow), their desire for personal success, responsibility and autonomy. In most formal organizations geared towards achieving objectives there are too few prospects for the fulfilment of such personal development goals. There are far too many inhibitive and restrictive conditions: control mechanisms, priorities imposed from outside, conflicts between short and long-term goals, payment mechanisms and other obligations, hierarchical demarcations, cost and efficiency considerations and much more.

Argyris

People look for:	Self-actualization, success, responsibility, autonomy
Organizations offer:	Dependence, control, obligation, conflict

For Argyris these clearly unavoidable, perhaps even natural conflicts explain the lack of motivation that he so often observed. It is not because people are naturally lazy and work-shy. Lack of motivation is an understandable response by any normal person to the generally limiting and frustrating conditions that organizations impose upon their members. People are in fact very well disposed and eager to be independent, responsible and autonomous. Most children at least are raised and encouraged to be so. However, the restrictions imposed by the structures, objectives and autonomous laws of the typical organization place people in an unnatural relationship of dependence and reduce them to childlike vulnerability, frustrating their struggle for autonomy.

In this way work becomes a necessary evil, instead of a source of contentment. Payment thus takes on the character of compensation for something abhorrent, instead of recognition for something positive.

Therefore, as with McGregor, Argyris also criticizes organizational inefficiency and the lack of opportunity or willingness to exploit the full potential of people in the organization. It can be concluded from his criticism that clear decision-making processes, open communication, information about necessary changes as well as defining clear areas of work and responsibility could reduce this frustrating organizational inefficiency. Rivalry and intrigue, gossip and awkward entanglements, nepotism and other irregularities are all additional tendencies that are often apparent and extremely detrimental to positive motivation. That such shortcomings shatter the fulfilment not only of personal goals but also of organizational ones is obvious. Nevertheless, attempts to address and improve this are frequently only piecemeal and short on success. This explains the evident criticism and also pessimism in Argyris and McGregor.

Both, however, devised their theories in the 1950s. If we find that today things are not quite so bad, then we have indeed learnt something over the years . . .

Herzberg

Perhaps the most influential, or at least the most well-known theory, that directly tackles motivation to work was developed by Frederick W.

Herzberg together with Mausner, Peterson, Capwell and others (*The Motivation to Work*, 1959).

Herzberg *et al.* carried out research that would later go down in the annals as the 'Pittsburgh Study'. The research aimed to find out which work situations and conditions were experienced positively and with enthusiasm, and which negatively or with despondency. The research was based on the statements of about 200 employees in technology and business, of whom all had had sound vocational training (engineers, accountants).

An analysis of the statements revealed two groups of factors that could trigger either satisfaction or dissatisfaction with aspects of work. These triggers, initially termed motivators and hygiene factors, gradually became known under various headings. *Motivators* and *hygiene factors* are not perhaps the most helpful of terms as they often lead to misunderstanding. Several years ago the author took part in a discussion during which it became evident that one of the participants (a manager) believed 'hygiene factors' actually referred to sanitary arrangements. These factors are also often described as 'satisfiers' and 'dissatisfiers'. The terms *intrinsic* and *extrinsic factors* are also used.

Whichever term may be preferred, the subject of study is always in the first instance the cause of work satisfaction, and in the second instance the trigger for dissatisfaction. It might well be suggested that merely stating that these phenomena exist is nothing new. Herzberg's vital contribution however is to describe the causes, which – as will become clear – is not an easy endeavour. At least as significant was the discovery that satisfaction and dissatisfaction can be said to run on two different tracks. This discovery acknowledged that shortcomings or particular circumstances may well lead to dissatisfaction, but that rectifying the shortcoming or alleviating the conditions does not necessarily lead to satisfaction; in fact this is very seldom the case. The people concerned may no longer be actively dissatisfied, but that does not yet equate to

---

Herzberg

| Motivators/intrinsic factors: | trigger satisfaction when fulfilled (e.g. challenges) |
| Hygiene factors/extrinsic factors: | trigger dissatisfaction when unfulfilled (e.g. pay) |

Hygiene factors cannot compensate for the lack of motivators.

Not being dissatisfied (unhappy) is not automatically tantamount to being satisfied (happy).

satisfaction. Terminology is very important in Herzberg's logic; unfortunately it is also the theory's Achilles heel. This primarily has to do with the choice of words, however, not the substance. If we use the word 'frustration' instead of dissatisfaction, and '(positive) motivation' instead of satisfaction, then it is perhaps clearer to understand.

Herzberg perceived that certain circumstances and work conditions, when poorly and inadequately structured, lead to dissatisfaction (frustration). Among other things this can concern administrative directives, regulations, processes of proposing and approving ideas, relationships with management and colleagues, information, communication, layout of the office, equipment, work intensity and – perhaps surprising for many – pay.

Although it is generally believed that pay is particularly important in releasing strong motivational forces, Herzberg's enquiries and analyses demonstrated that this is not the case. The author can reinforce this unreservedly after decades of experience. It is, however, undisputed that poor or unfair pay has a dissatisfying effect. This dissatisfaction can grow and finally like a fungus envelop someone's entire attitude towards the work, the job and the business. This results in complete dissatisfaction, frustration and a negative frame of mind. If, however, a superior pays wisely, the dissatisfaction (frustration) will be overcome. That does not, however, automatically guarantee satisfaction (positive motivation). Not being dissatisfied means exactly what it says, nothing more. Even in everyday conversation a subtler, but clearer distinction is made. If someone responds to an enquiry about their well-being with 'I am not unhappy', that means something completely different to 'I am happy'.

Dissatisfaction and frustration on the one hand, satisfaction and motivation on the other, run therefore on two different tracks or – to put it more pompously – on two separate 'continua'. The one track leads from dissatisfaction to not being dissatisfied, the other from not being satisfied to satisfaction. Hence being free of pay concerns means not being dissatisfied, which is certainly desirable as that precludes the risk that the fungus of dissatisfaction will spread (so long as no other dissatisfaction triggers are active). In this sense the term 'hygiene factor' is wholly apt.

Herzberg also discovered which are the 'motivators' or the triggers of satisfaction. The analysis of the responses to his survey showed that more important than 'external' considerations, or *hygiene factors*, was the quality of the work itself, the 'inner factors' or *intrinsic factors*. Typical examples of this are success, recognition (by colleagues, superiors, other employees within the business or experts outside it), being challenged, the sense of making a worthwhile contribution, trust, independence, the chance of career development, opportunities to go on vocational training and responsibility. These and similar factors generate real satisfaction and positive motivation. An absence of *motivators* is worse than having under-developed *hygiene factors*. Far more serious than 'only' being dissatisfied with one extrinsic factor or another, a lack of motivation and satisfaction has a gravely negative impact on attitudes towards work and also towards the business. Lack of motivation leads to a drop in performance, inner withdrawal, and in most cases also to leaving the business.

The logic of Herzberg's conclusions affords a useful practical guide. It makes plain sense to avoid dissatisfaction by ensuring that 'extrinsic' factors, the hygiene factors, are under control. Although it is more difficult to acti-vate and optimize the *motivators*, the effort is justified by the high levels of motivation that can be achieved.

The fact that Herzberg's survey was conducted almost 50 years ago is palpable. His conclusions in particular clearly belong to the environment of their time. In the 1950s the significance of hierarchy was far greater than it is now; the roles of leaders and led were much more sharply accen-tuated; the 'dependent employee' was actually far more dependent and passive; open communication and criticism were much less pronounced than in our considerably more emancipated culture. The guiding principle was 'top–down'; 'bottom–up' approaches hardly existed. In most busi-nesses workers were far more reliant than now on '*being* motivated'. Today, the person who passively sits and waits, neither seeking nor enhancing his 'motivators', is ill-advised.

McClelland

David McClelland (*The Achieving Society*, 1961) developed another inter-esting theory about motivation. 'Achievement' is performance that pro-duces something: the work, the completion (of a task). McClelland takes the position that much of our behaviour is developed and 'learnt' from childhood, through education, experience, reward or punishment (that is, through positive or negative feedback). These processes of learning and gathering experience nurture particular needs, which reside between the conscious and subconscious, regulating behaviour so that they are satis-fied. Because very young people must deal with the cultural, social and also the economic environment in one way or another, they learn that cer-tain modes of behaviour are more successful than others. Since these modes bring rewards, the particular needs associated with them are rein-forced and become 'ingrained'; thus there is a behavioural cycle in which needs that are ingrained by rewards lead to patterns of behaviour that in turn produce greater rewards.

Relating his theory to the working world and to motivation levels, McClelland offers three key needs that regulate behaviour. These are:

- *The need for achievement:* The need to reach goals, to accomplish something, to overcome difficulties, to prove one's strength (not only physical, but above all mental and intellectual), to push oneself.
- *The need for power:* This need elicits behaviour that should influence, persuade or control others. It requires personal ideas and goals to be passed on to others through dominating behaviour. In order to satisfy the need to establish and secure authority, there is an endeavour to influence opinions, to control all resources for work (especially information!) and to hold sway over decision-making processes concerning work or business objectives.
- *The need for affiliation:* The need to belong, to be a member of a group or a team; to form and maintain good interpersonal relations; to be socially acknowledged as 'successful' or 'likable'.

Although everybody possesses these three keys needs, their intensity varies enormously from person to person.

The most important need in terms of working behaviour and motivation levels is the *need for achievement*. People who attach value to achieving goals, results or high levels of performance evince certain characteristic behaviour patterns. They value independence, they want to work on their own initiative, be innovative and creative. Hence they look for challenges and are willing to take risks, although not without realistically assessing them first. They need tasks that are difficult yet not impossible. For these people it is the work, the fulfilment of the task itself, that affords the most satisfaction. Pay is not so much an aim in itself, but a measure of performance.

McClelland's theory is revealing for it suggests that the way these three key needs are developed and interrelate can lay bare a variety of attitudes towards the fulfilment of different tasks. A particularly strong sense of the need for achievement would indicate above all a person very well disposed towards expert, challenging and innovative work that makes a high demand on professional initiative. An acute need for power suggests the desire for a leadership role and the likelihood that this will be well performed. The need for affiliation, the need to belong socially, seems to be a sound basis for predominantly team-oriented work in which the task is more important than the individual.

The variously distinctive ways in which the three key needs evolve can often be illustrated not only by educational and career development, but also by private desires and leisure activities, and this can further be verified through interviews. Test methods can also be applied, using, for

---

McClelland

Successful behaviour is conditioned through 'ingrained' needs:

Need for achievement → Performance
Need for power → Responsibility
Need for affiliation → Teamwork

---

example, the *Thematic Apperception Test* (TAT), whereby the interpretation of graphic descriptions and of the elaborations of given subjects can provide relevant insights to the trained eye. From McClelland's point of view it is useful for everyone concerned to know how the three key needs contribute to individual profiles. In this way the basis of successful work-placement can be established and 'the right person can get the right job'.

Because the three needs are not rooted in human nature but are 'learnt', as illustrated above, they trigger behaviour that is felt to be successful and rewarding. It is therefore vital that at work, too, there is continuous positive feedback. This might occur on the one hand through the way in which tasks complement the individual configuration of needs. On the other hand, as a clear and immediately understandable confirmation of success, pay can also help partly satisfy the needs. Behaviour that has been rewarded in both immaterial and material respects will be perceived to be justified and will be repeated.

Vroom

The *VIE-Theory* (Valence–Instrumentality–Expectancy) put forward by Victor H. Vroom (*Work and Motivation*, 1964) is in some respects related to McClelland's ideas.

Vroom, however, does not believe that fixed key needs exist, even ones with individually variable intensities. Rather he believes that individuals choose from various courses of action, depending on which is most likely to yield success. In effect, people opt for the course of action that corresponds to their own notions of the practicality, usefulness and probability of achieving the desired result. This forms the basis of the three pillars of Vroom's theory:

- Valence means value. This denotes how desirable the end result of an action or activity is.
- Instrumentality means assistance or collaboration. This describes the degree of effectiveness of the chosen action or activity, measuring it against the end result.

> **Vroom**
> Valence: An important personal goal.
> Instrumentality: A milestone on the way to reaching this goal.
> Expectancy: The probability that this milestone can be reached.
> Positive V, I and E → positive motivation

- Expectancy means expectation, prospect, hope. It expresses how high the probability is that the chosen action or activity will have the desired result.

Assuming that in each scenario there are a number of options, these three factors offer an explanation of why people are motivated to certain courses of action. Thus when the possibility arises to put in an exceptional performance, to take on additional tasks, to start a new project, then the thought-processes could go something like this:

- 'I would like to prove my competence so that I might be considered for promotion.' This is positive valence. The wish to tackle something new and additional thus complies with personal targets and ambition.
- 'I believe that this task is just what I am looking for to prove my ability to take on more demanding tasks.' This demonstrates a positive estimation of instrumentality, or the assistance it may give in reaching a personal goal to enhance career development.
- 'I believe I can successfully accomplish this task.' This expresses the expectation that one can in fact undertake and achieve the immediate goal or task. It is nevertheless a crucial requirement that the more important personal goal can be achieved, for this was the trigger (the real motive) for deciding to take on supplementary tasks in the first place.

If just one of the three criteria in this train of thought is judged negatively, then reason and logic should prevail and decide against undertaking the additional tasks.

This example shows vividly that it may be not only inappropriate but also misleading to see certain behaviour as 'unmotivated'. When someone decides against taking on additional tasks after rational consideration, then that person indeed has a motive, is therefore motivated. In such a case it would be important to find out the reason for the decision. There might be very sound reasons or there might be a misunderstanding. Perhaps the person concerned underestimates his or her own abilities and 'sleeping' talents could be awakened for the benefit of all. Finding out the cause can help provide the stimulus for change when someone really lacks ambition or is unwilling to take risks when innovation, dynamism and creativity are required. This helps to preclude later conflicts; discussion can be carried out on a more concrete, rational and less emotional basis, and this would inevitably be to the advantage of all.

By reflecting on these observations it can be seen that once again we are dealing with a theory of some practical relevance.

Locke, Latham

The pioneering work of Edwin A. Locke (*Toward a Theory of Task Motivation and Incentives*, 1968) is interesting in both theoretical and practical terms. It draws together personal targets and related moral concepts and value judgements to explain behaviour and motivation in work. Generally speaking Locke assumes the position that value judgements are formed on the basis of what is considered worth pursuing. Goals are drawn up from these aims or desires, which in turn, in order to be fulfilled, provide the spur for definite action. The degree of fulfilment is ultimately assessed and if necessary the original moral concepts are qualified or adjusted.

With direct reference to working behaviour, goals can raise both motivation and performance levels. The more demanding the goal, the higher the performance exerted to achieve it. There is the additional fact that goals signal clearly that an important issue is at stake, a priority for the business. This can establish a strong concentration of effort and drive towards these goals. Furthermore, goal setting will facilitate progress control by both the employees and the managers involved; this will enhance levels of performance. It is crucial that goals are not dictated unilaterally from 'above' but are agreed upon, for the willingness to perform depends among other things on whether performance expectations have been accepted.

Further research (E. A. Locke and G. P. Latham, *A Theory of Goal Setting and Task Performance*, 1990) emphasized specifically the importance of agreeing upon goals. Such agreement can ensure that workers identify with the goal, which in turn can engender an increased feeling of commitment to achieving set targets.

Locke, Latham

Personal moral concepts → drawing up corresponding goals → identification with the goals → achieving the goals → positive feedback → more challenging goals → increased effort

---

Equivalence and Dissonance

In our *tour d'horizon* we have become familiar with needs, expectations, objectives and many related factors and elements that determine motivation – or frustration.

There is an additional factor that can play a positive or negative role, namely fairness, equivalence or equality. In their working lives – and in their private lives – people are continually searching for confirmation that success stands in a harmonious relationship with effort. When this is not so, then tension results. This can have a thoroughly 'demotivating', and therefore frustrating, effect.

If it is felt, when looking at individual circumstances, that a great deal is being given but very little is being received in return, then 'cognitive dissonance' arises (L. Festinger, *A Theory of Cognitive Dissonance*, 1957). This is an unpleasant or even unacceptable experience, and every effort will be made either to establish a more balanced relationship or to escape from the unsatisfactory situation.

It has often been demonstrated that in practice this type of cognitive dissonance is thoroughly subjective and rarely reflects objectively veri-fiable facts. In the main such feelings are based upon comparisons that are certainly not always relevant. Self-evaluations of performance or of career potential sometimes overestimate the individual's performance, while the contributions of other – supposedly comparable – people are frequently underestimated, or vice versa. Whichever way around this happens, cognitive dissonance with all its unhappy side effects is not far off. The same often also applies to comparisons of pay: not only might the information on which such comparisons are made be incom-plete or misleading, but also those chosen for comparison may have been selected quite arbitrarily and unrealistically. Thus hasty conclu-sions will sometimes be drawn: 'If this person (whose talents are well below mine) earns so much, then it is obvious that I am underpaid.' Because individual notions of fairness, equivalence or equality are not based wholly on absolutes (one's own career, own pay), but on relative factors (comparison with others), this can augment feelings of negative motivation.

Equivalence and dissonance
Fairness/proportionality is desirable → motivates
Unfairness/disproportionality will be rejected → frustrates

Regardless of whether the feeling of injustice or disproportion is right or wrong, investigating the causes for it is vital. This will happen best where open discussion is promoted or made possible, where there is transparency of appraisal and pay criteria, where feedback on performance and development potential is offered, and where there is an endeavour to talk in all areas with objectivity and professionalism.

'Sixteen Basic Desires'

This chapter has so far attempted to give a broad overview of the most varied investigations into the motivation to work. Maslow's theory of the Pyramid of Needs, now decades old, began the overview. It is useful by way of rounding off to make brief reference to the research of Steven Reiss, who concluded from his very broad empirical studies conducted in the United States, Canada and Japan that there are 16 motives that determine behaviour (Steven Reiss, *Who am I? The Sixteen Desires that Motivate our Behavior and Define our Personality*, 2000).

These 16 'desires' relate to the factors that determine human behaviour, giving it a purpose. This purpose is established in the attempt to fulfil the 16 desires (wishes, needs, yearnings). Hence Reiss does not talk first of the causes, but of the wishes that give our motivation, our behaviour and ultimately our personality their very own character.

According to Reiss's research, the 16 desires are present in everybody; most of them are genetically anchored, while some are also acquired through learning and social processes. The intensity of each desire, however, varies from person to person. This theory gains credence from the fact that it underpins many conclusions gained from experience, namely that people possess their own key to motivation. Motivation 'techniques', therefore, are at their best founded on 'trial and error' and at their worst manipulative, even if they are not meant to be.

Motives of behaviour arise, according to Reiss, from the following 16 desires:

- power
- independence
- curiosity
- acceptance
- order
- saving

- honour
- idealism
- social contact
- family
- status
- vengeance
- romance
- eating
- physical activity
- tranquillity.

These terms are not paraphrased as they speak for themselves.

Reiss does not see these desires as a hierarchical relationship in the way that Maslow views needs.

The needs identified by Reiss (perhaps not all, but certainly most of them) can undoubtedly have a great impact on behaviour in the working environment and thus on the motivation to work. It is superfluous to state that not all of these terms are new, for this is not to be expected. Power and affiliation (social contact in Reiss) were there with McClelland, nourishment and activity with Maslow, and other connections can be similarly made. Reiss's term 'independence' comprises among other things autonomy and self-actualization, and it is precisely these that play a dominant role in the motivation to work.

Reiss's observations, which after all are still very recent ones, will certainly shed a great deal of light yet on motivation in particular: its crucial issues and how it is managed.

This is a good point to close this overview of most of the important theories, hypotheses and ideas, which have also been interesting in terms of their practical implications, and conclude the theme of the motivation to work. It would not be possible to outline further theories of motivation without the subject getting out of hand and risking repetition. The theories we have considered were selected on entirely subjective criteria, mainly on the basis of the author's decades of experience, which provided the opportunity to test many of the implications in practice, to observe and judge them.

Eight Points for Reflection

1. The various theories make an important contribution to understanding the phenomenon of 'motivation'. None of them, however, offers a

comprehensive explanation of what really generates motivation or how it can be managed.

2. Hence there are no definitive 'motivation techniques', or reliably effective methods that can be applied to everybody in all possible situations.

3. Examining the different theories, hypotheses and ideas, however, leads to a measure of understanding. This can be extremely helpful in forming management principles, communication methods, performance appraisals, the setting and agreement of objectives, payment policies, personnel development, career strategies and other relevant elements governing the management of the business and personnel or human resource policies.

4. The aim is not to choose one of many possible theories and put it into practice. It is better to understand the diverse ideas and to personalize them through intellectual reworking. In this way personal concepts can be formed to suit various fluctuations in both internal and external circumstances and demands.

5. Looking back on the last four decades, it is clear that a lot has been learnt and that a pragmatic relationship between theory and practice has in the main been very fruitful.

6. Moving from hierarchical structures to those based on participation, from authoritative or paternalistic management styles to those based on communication and consensus has been successfully tackled, and insights into positive motivation have been more strongly integrated into the practice of management.

7. Economic and social changes over the last 20 years have indeed been pervasive and dramatic on a scale never before witnessed. Just some of the key terms that have characterized deeply penetrating changes are: internationalization or the globalization of markets; restructuring; business mergers; joint ventures; strategic alliances; information technology; virtualization; relocations; reorientation, ranging from diversification strategies to core business strategies; outsourcing; displacement of the 'old economy' by the 'new economy', and subsequent disillusionment with the latter. The potential for motivation crises and problems of frustration was immense. In spite of this, many and indeed most of these changes, even those concerning new questions of motivation, were overcome successfully.

8. It is clear that as far as the present and the future are concerned, the emphasis in motivation has moved away from passive expectation and towards the active input and initiative of the individual. Motivation is no longer predominantly 'forced happiness' insisted upon by the leadership as their debt to the 'employees', but forms part of the individual's

responsibility for successfully developing career and life opportunities. In the independence of a post-hierarchical society, long-term ties to an employer and passive expectation are continually being replaced by flexibility, active drawing up of career outlines, increased information and awareness. Alongside this, the traditional capital-based motivation for running a business is also evolving into a force that has significant bearing on a company's success.

Conclusion: Significant Elements of Motivation

The following selection of points is not intended to add yet another theory of motivation to the many that already exist, but to draw from existing theories and practices elements of motivation that are generally applicable and relevant.

- All individuals hold the key to their own desires, motives and motivation. It is therefore meaningless to say 'according to Herzberg you should now be motivated'. However, motivation does at least require:
  - necessity and need (what must be done, will be done)
  - involvement in action and result
  - promise of reward and recognition
  - integration of the activity with personal life and experience
  - challenging work content and demands.

- In working life just as in life in general a healthy mixture of *drama, ritual and routine* is important. Drama on its own (struggle, competition, argument, harassment, deadline pressure) is destructive – for some sooner, for others later – because eventually everyone can become burnt out. Routine alone may be comfortable, but eventually it kills all initiative and creativity and thereby takes all joy out of the activity. One can usually identify people who are only occupied in routine work. Ritual, in the sense of unendingly repetitive action that has more ceremonial than productive value, may offer stability and security, but without anything else paralysis, introspection and the quest for *l'art pour l'art* (art for art's sake) follow quickly. A healthy mixture is thus important. This mixture, however, varies immensely from person to person, a fact that can also often explain different career preferences. Leaving aside the fact that different skills are needed for different jobs, much also depends on individual requirements for drama, ritual and routine. These determine whether someone pursues a career as an international manager, university lecturer, lawyer, business adviser, clerk, salesperson or self-employed businessman. There are clearly certain needs that influence the reasoning behind decisions.

- *Management style* has a lot to do with motivation. To some extent it is bound up with time and culture. Decades ago an authoritative management style reflected expectations in a strictly hierarchical framework and offered generally stable order and security; today such an attitude would be extremely counterproductive. In today's world we look for information, cooperation, openness, involvement with decision-making processes, consensus and sharing of responsibility.

- The *strong need for personal development and self-actualization* requires that work should not be experienced ultimately as a mechanical process within an incomprehensibly huge machine, but as a contribution to business objectives, as recognized performance, as success and confirmation of personal and professional competence. It in no way contradicts this desire for personal growth that most people also have a need for belonging – to a business, a group or a profession, at least to something that imparts a positive value, including security, status and prestige.

- Once again we hit upon the importance of *reward and recognition* for motivation. Here, these terms refer not only to payment or any type of financial remuneration, but to 'rewards' in the broadest sense. These include rewards extending beyond financial considerations, such as career development, increase of knowledge, extension of responsibility, inclusion in important advisory and decision-making committees within and also outside the business (for example by representing interest groups, lobby organizations or a field of experts).

- To conclude, there is an important point concerning organization structure, in terms of:

-   definition of areas of responsibility
-   clarity of role description
-   transparency of decision-making processes
-   feedback over successes and failures
-   exchange of knowledge, experience and know-how
-   shared learning.

Clarity over these details of structure improves organizational efficiency and thereby releases the energy that people must otherwise expend on finding their way through a labyrinth of muddy priorities, overlaps, duplications, contradictory goals and other notoriously frustrating obstacles.

Tools of Management

New ideas and tools of management have been developed from decades of management theories and practices. This has been particularly marked since the 1950s, when the opportunity for major economic growth coincided with a shortage of qualified workers who could give businesses a decisive advantage. The post-colonial era was now clearly taking hold and markets were becoming more international and competitive, business strategies more diversified, and social and ethical responsibilities more demanding. The demands on the management apparatus were therefore growing.

These ideas and methods are particularly significant in terms of working behaviour and the motivation to work. Here those which are immediately relevant to people will be singled out.

Evaluation and Pay

Two of the most important tools, namely appraisal of performance and potential, and reward strategies and incentive systems, will be specifically discussed in Parts II and III.

There is in addition a whole host of tools that can have a positive or negative effect on motivation, depending on the care given to preparing for their introduction and the way they are used.

Management by Objectives: Target Agreement

In the discussion of motivation theories frequent reference has already been made to the importance of setting and agreeing upon objectives. Drawing up and pursuing business objectives is probably as old as the institution of business itself. Not quite so old – even if no longer completely novel – is the integration of objectives in the practice of management and motivation. Many will be familiar with the term 'Management by Objectives' (MbO). The end of the 1960s saw the author's first acquaintance with the term in practical test-runs and implementations.

> Management by objectives transforms goals: from the level of planning, expectation, hope or outline to an element that has binding force, engagement, and commitment, one that has been discussed and agreed upon at every level in the business.

MbO was then something new and progressive, but it was a child of its time: the target setting process was clearly vertical, from top to bottom. Nevertheless for the first time discussion of the reasons for choosing and quantifying objectives was institutionalized. Moreover, by formulating sub-targets that deviated from the main business objectives, it was possible to factor in a range of considerations that directly reflected the motivations and concerns of individuals.

> Target setting gradually took on more of the nature of an agreement, reflecting the development of a management style based on participation, gravitating away from hierarchical structures to more balanced and strategic organization and to planning processes which were progressively synthesising 'top-down' with 'bottom-up' approaches.
>
> All the while MbO remained the essence and origin. There are few professionally run businesses today in which target setting and agreement do not play a significant role.

MbO also allows or at least simplifies a host of other measures. Thus it frequently marked the beginning of professional, task-related communication between superior and subordinate. It helped to place performance appraisal on a professional and objective basis. This also enabled performance-related reward policies to be more transparent and easier to understand.

Gradually there were of course many further developments, improvements, sometimes even just simple alterations, but in the main prodigious advances were made in the quality of target setting, in the relevance and

In the town of Ch... there lived the famous archer Francis T... He had a secret: he would shoot first and then paint the target!

credibility of evaluations, and in the transparency and objectification of determining wages. It is quite right that further exploration in MbO should continue, for circumstances too will continue to change. One need only consider how hugely significant objectives are for the efficiency of incentive systems, which today are employed far more widely than ever before.

The concerns of MbO include cost efficiency as well as credibility and motivation – or at least the avoidance of frustration.

Openness and Transparency

Knowing how to direct what Herzberg calls the 'hygiene factors' – the principles, rules, methods and tools of both management and human resource policies – was in the past mostly the preserve of the management levels and those responsible for and concerned with areas of expertise. This reflected the predominantly hierarchical structures and generally paternalistic character of the management style of the time. However, this generated mistrust and misunderstanding and fostered a degree of pettifoggery and machination in a culture of secrecy. There was really nothing sinister that had to be kept hidden. The tradition of withholding information and avoiding discussion, however, was seen as crucial in maintaining management and decision-making privileges, and in preserving authority, which otherwise would have been seen to be in jeopardy.

The 1968 student rebellion, now long consigned to the history books, emitted signals that led some businesses to re-examine the policy of silence about principles and methods that immediately concerned employees and their interests. The author himself took part in such discussions when he worked at the heart of a large business. The question was raised as to whether the 'closed book' policy was appropriate in the light of the fact that in a few years time many of the students who stood on the barricades in Paris or took to the streets in other leading university towns against stagnation, authority claims, institutions and the establishment would, as graduates of economics faculties, form the next generation of managers. It was clear that the insurgents of 1968 were not mere crazy revolutionaries nor simply bent on provocation. To the careful observer it was evident that these events heralded the end of an era and the dawn of a new cultural and social philosophy. The 'long march through the institutions' did indeed take place later, albeit less spectacularly than some of its protagonists had imagined, but nevertheless extremely effectively.

In a few businesses at first, and subsequently in more and more, there was a vigorous movement towards open communication. Thus people could find out for example what rules governed pay policy, how various jobs were assessed, the criteria by which performance was appraised or how employees came to be considered for a change of job or promotion. Once information about principles and methods was released, details relating to individuals were made accessible.

For many, indeed for the great majority, this was both interesting and positively motivating: the frustrating guessing game as to how, why and where one was placed was finally over. For some it was certainly also embarrassing and unwelcome, and a few – mainly the older members of management – saw it as unnecessary tinkering and a weakening of authority. The key issue for what was then a new policy of openness and transparency was not to establish individual or collective platforms for negotiation, but to pass on information in the expectation and hope of strengthening trust. The policy of openness became indisputable and it should remain so, even in the face of the occasional temptation to avoid certain procedures that bring with them a risk of criticism.

Information and Communication

Openness and transparency do not only concern human resource principles and systems. They are about engaging the workers at every level in developments and decisions. In contrast to Taylor's time, when people were virtually part of a conveyer belt process, personal initiative, autonomy and creativity are now required. These are activated through positive desires and motives. Awareness of the business objectives, or of the specific business department, knowledge of the markets, the state of the competition, technological developments, expectations and strategies for the future are crucial for this activation. Such information may be more easily made accessible in small firms or businesses than in large organizations. On the other hand large businesses have more means at their disposal to put information systems in place efficiently. One must certainly guard against the belief that it is enough to send out letters to workers or disseminate news through internal e-mail systems. These means of distributing information are useful, but do not go far enough. What is lacking is above all the personal touch and direct intercourse.

In the 1990s the author had the opportunity to work out an information concept in a large international company, which has since been implemented more intensively year after year. Starting with the top management, the flow of information meanders down to the lowest level, through all the business departments (encompassing in total more than 200,000 workers in many countries and all continents). The information looks both backwards and forwards in time, and the content is categorized according to different key areas that correspond to specific departments. Furthermore, at every stage there are details about over-arching areas and also about the business as a whole. The highest level of management in a specific area presents the information. The nature of the process lent the concept its name of the 'Cascade System'.

A comprehensive, institutionalized information system creates the frame-work for fluid and targeted information and communication with the work-ers in the various business departments. This will also facilitate direct involvement in processes of change and decision making. This in turn generates unity, engagement and commitment, and makes the work both more interesting and more efficient.

Information, communication and involvement of the workers – both as individuals and as working groups – represent a form of cooperation. They should not be confused with rights to information, advice or consultation stipulated by legal regulations or works committees. These have their own function and are subject to different rules of the game.

Job Design

The more interesting the task or the greater the challenge, the more intense will be the desire to accomplish it successfully. Positive motivation ener-gies can further be released through the organization of the task, the *job design*. There has over the course of time been a great deal of change here too, mostly for the better.

In the past only the upper management levels enjoyed interesting, demanding tasks. In the lower levels job content was in general narrowly defined. It was fragmented into the smallest possible units, comprising mostly monotonous tasks at fixed and strictly defined work stations. The work was subject to rigorous and often constant control. The organiza-tional structure had many levels of responsibility and a pronounced hier-archical emphasis. Many of these levels, especially in the lower and mid-dle levels of management, were mainly there to supervise, to compare, to analyse, to summarize, to report 'to the top', to make recommendations and to give orders 'to the lower ranks'. It was not unusual for businesses to have a dozen or more organizational levels one on top of the other.

In these circumstances there was little room for independence, initiative, creative freedom, indeed anything that generates pleasure in work or moti-vates from within – Herzberg's *intrinsic motivation*. More and more was gradually done to counteract this, for example through programmes such as *job enrichment* and *job enlargement*. These terms will certainly still be fresh in the memory, so they require only a brief explanation:

- *Job enrichment* means enriching the job content through supplementary tasks, helping to break up too much order and routine – providing more drama!

- *Job enlargement* means broadening very narrowly defined, specialized work by adding related but nevertheless different tasks.

In addition, a more straightforward organizational structure superseded previous complexity. This not only enabled swifter and more direct communication, but also shut down excessive control and unproductive bureaucracy. Often-excessive specialization was replaced by bringing together logically related tasks. There had been a time when the actual production process was kept strictly distinct from maintenance and quality control, which had their own specialists; it was unthinkable for the machine operator to carry out initial quality control tests, or carry out immediate overhaul and maintenance work to correct a fault. What was then unthinkable because it contradicted prevailing concepts of control and duty has now become the norm.

A great deal has been learnt in the meantime: quality circles, autonomous working groups, total productive maintenance, *empowerment*. The latter term has degenerated into something of a catchword, but it signifies one of the steps made in gaining ground for greater independence and individual responsibility on a level previously reserved for the 'top' executives.

Development and Training

The pursuit of further development is a powerful motive for human activity. That applies just as much, and perhaps above all, to the working world. Investment in personal development is, therefore, not only necessary in encouraging talents and abilities to keep apace of continually changing and largely growing demands, but also constitutes an important motivator.

> Gaining career experience, getting professional qualifications, expert training and personal development are at least as important for the workers as good pay.

An efficient career plan is vital to harvest the fruits of these training and development efforts. It is naturally in the interests of the business, just as in those of the workers, not to allow performance potential to go unharnessed.

The 'job for life' is no longer guaranteed anywhere; even in Japan the celebrated 'life-long employment' has long since had its day. Thus, in an era that demands adaptation and flexibility, great value must constantly be attached to further training and development both to encourage motivation and also to secure an existence.

Employability may have become a catchword, but it expresses a crucial issue: the opportunity to market knowledge and skills acquired in one company to find employment if necessary with another, or to be self-employed for a longer or shorter period of time.

In the short term, training, development and career planning may seem a decided luxury from the business's point of view, for changes can happen frequently and quickly, calling into question the soundness of these measures. However, it can hardly be a serious alternative simply to do nothing and leave everything to chance. There is no choice but to try to act better and more purposefully and – as a necessary concession to the increasingly short life spans of knowledge, experience and techniques – to condense the training schedules.

Training and development (and also the now somewhat hackneyed and outdated sounding 'management development') are vital investments in raising worker competence, are important motivators and – let us not forget – often also make a business particularly attractive for the most talented people.

Motivation and Incentive

To close this chapter on motivation, let us recall that many different theories and hypotheses have been embraced, described and explained. This was followed by an attempt to draw the various strands together and finally establish their practical relevance.

It has been shown that the assorted abstractions and concepts about motivation are in no way confined to 'pure theory'; on the contrary, application in real life shows that many of the insights gained on a scientific and empirical basis afford useful ideas for practical implementation.

Furthermore, it is important to note that, in its triggering of particular patterns of behaviour and activating desires, motivation is ultimately a highly personal matter: every individual has a distinct pattern of motivation. There may indeed be principles and contexts that apply generally, but these should not be exercised indiscriminately. Hence specific motivation 'techniques' are not to be recommended; if only in order to avoid the dangerous ground of manipulation.

The more that is known about the essence of motivation, the more effectively one can 'motivate' in leadership and action. This is not only the preserve of management; it concerns everybody. All individuals can contribute to their own motivation – and indeed do so, whether specifically and consciously or intuitively and subconsciously.

Motivation will always exist because there will always be new desires in one form or another: whether to do something, to avoid something, not to do something, to engage in something, to behave impartially, to oppose, to look for something new, to hold on to the past, to fight, to defend, to withdraw . . . Motivation is eternal. Like a catalyst, it influences process, but exhausts no energies itself.

> Motivation should not be confused with incentive. Incentive is specific, more short than long-term and is based largely on a specifically designated promise of reward for a level of performance that is just as specifically determined. It can also be a threatened punishment.

If a sufficiently high bonus is promised for achieving a particularly high sales figure, then the agents will put in a great deal of effort to earn this bonus. If on the other hand there is the threat that the five worst agents will lose their jobs, then everyone will endeavour not to be counted among them. Neither case, however, concerns motivation, but rather incentive, a stimulus, which ceases to exist the moment the activity stops. We see motivation at work where an agent, even without the promise of a bonus, tries to be the best because high performance reflects his need for achievement, one of the acquired needs identified by McClelland. Or indeed, as Vroom's VIE-theory suggests, because the agent hopes that his endeavours will help him to achieve a distant goal, such as promotion to head sales representative.

Motivation can be positive or negative. In both cases it has a lasting impact precisely because it feeds off needs and desires, which – at least for people in the working world – not only relate to final outcomes, but also and most significantly to the organization and content of work, tasks, areas of responsibility and additional duties.

The term motivation encompasses much more than mere incentive. Motivation is the combination of different desires that direct and influence behaviour and action. It is also the context and area in which one type of behaviour might be emphasized, encouraged and aroused, and another suppressed, interrupted or forestalled. Of course motives release certain stimulants, but these do not generate desire but rather are a consequence of it.

> Incentive in the sense of bonus and reward does not bypass motivation, but is rather directly linked to it by way of a short-cut, making a predetermined

reward directly dependent upon a certain level of performance. It is thus entirely superfluous to debate, as some people do, whether incentive systems motivate or not. They do not, because they cannot; instead they do other things, such as encourage certain levels of performance, independent of the degree of motivation.

Discussing this theme during one of his lectures, the author undertook a harmless experiment. He asked which of his students would, for quite an insignificant amount of money, be prepared to remove their left shoe, wave it with the right hand over their heads, leave the lecture theatre and enter the nearby refectory still waving the shoe. The take-up was overwhelming. Does this have anything to do with motivation? Surely not, if one rejects the idea that this is a form of the need to acquire money to fulfil physiological primary needs as Maslow discussed. It is simply an example of an incentive. This runs like clockwork, with the action resulting from a trade-off in which the exertion for the required deed (D) is balanced against the promised reward (R). When R is more highly valued than D, D is accomplished; when not, D remains unfulfilled.

Generally, the incentive to do something does not only arise from the hope of financial reward (this also applies to the world of work). The promise of public recognition for exceptional performance can be a considerable stimulus, even if this recognition is only the award of a certificate that has no monetary value whatsoever. Take the case where the most successful sales agent in one particular quarter is permitted to drive a special model for the next three months rather than the usual company car. That is no great financial incentive, but it is externally visible and gives that person a higher status. The opportunity to attain such acknowledgement can be a stronger incentive than a financial bonus.

Incentive is not the same as motivation, nor can it supplant it. Where challenges are lacking, where there is little opportunity to show initiative, where creative talents are not encouraged, where routine takes the upper hand, in those cases work becomes a necessary evil to earn a living.

In these circumstances people look for other outlets for their unexploited talents and abilities. This partly explains why many people often put in a great deal of effort and even undergo considerable hardship outside their jobs in order to find challenges and satisfaction in, for example, voluntary work for charitable institutions, environmental protection, community projects, or assisting with youth organizations. These and many other activities are undertaken, typically without pay or, often, reimbursement of expenses, so that people not only give their energy and time, but often also their money.

What leads someone to take up an offer that roughly translates as 'a job on an island in the Russian Arctic or the forests of tropical Thailand or the savannah of Zimbabwe; accommodation in a hut or tent for several people; basic but adequate food; physically difficult and dangerous work; no pay; all travel, transport and insurance costs to be paid by yourself; working day of at least ten hours'. That does not exactly sound like an attractive job offer; neither is it. Yet it appeals to voluntary workers who have to give up their holidays, money and perhaps even their health, in order to work on projects such as the environment or animal welfare. One typical example can be found at www.ecovolunteers.org.

Do these opportunities only attract free-spirited adventurers with unlimited resources of time and money? Absolutely not: many of these people have entirely 'normal' jobs and lead a thoroughly 'civilized' life. But they are certainly missing challenge and innovation, creativity and self-determined, independent action; they see too little result, too little opportunity for development and too much saturation: in other words, their motivation potential is far from being harnessed. Work as an 'ecovolunteer', in contrast to their daily life, offers plenty of room for motivation.

Motivation is a fundamental attitude, which is in turn initiated by desires and 'motives'. It is all-embracing and determines trends, objectives and even, if you will, entire life aims. Work – whatever form it may take – plays a significant but not exclusive role. Motivation influences or even determines fundamental philosophies towards work. This is what we mean when we speak of the 'motivation to work'. It is governed by different needs, whether acquired or inherited, by various internal or external factors, by the desire for personal development and balance, and by numerous other elements that have been mentioned in connection with the different motivation theories.

Motivation to work is thus an integral element of what constitutes an individual's entire motivation. It would therefore be misleading to view it as a single entity that can be isolated and 'manipulated'. Certainly when people speak of the motivation to work they often mean quite simply the incentive to work represented by a promised reward or pressure. Because motivation and incentive are not the same, because they are subject to different rules and because they differ immensely from each other in their effect, the two are dealt with separately in this book.

Incentive systems will be discussed in detail towards the end of the section on reward strategies.

Evaluation of Performance and Potential

CHAPTER 2

Performance Appraisal

Sense and Purpose

The point of performance appraisals is to see if the people under contract are performing as well as they can, and also to assess whether they are being fairly rewarded (their remuneration, like their duties, is subject to contractual agreement). This limits evaluations to the level of concrete, or at least verifiable, facts. However, there are numerous relevant factors that, although they may only be indirectly related to performance, should nevertheless not be underestimated. These additional factors will, either officially or unofficially, play a part in evaluations. They include how the performance level was reached, whether the conditions were favourable or unfavourable, which abilities, strengths or weaknesses emerged on the day, whether similar, higher or lower levels of performance could be expected or encouraged in the future, what feedback would be sensible or perhaps even timely, whether the person concerned should be encouraged or held back, whether some specific performance has perhaps been achieved at the cost of other work. These considerations and countless others besides play a more or less palpable role.

Evaluation is not in any sense a phenomenon unique to the world of work. On the contrary, forming judgements, assessing other people, situations, possibilities, expectations, threats, opportunities and dangers is such an integral part of our lives that it is self-evident that people cannot live without evaluating. It is a crucial part of human survival strategies. We have constantly to judge and evaluate, making decisions not only in our careers but in every aspect of our lives about what we should do, what we should not do or which options we should choose. Sometimes it is very difficult to make the right choice. It is also not always easy to have all the relevant criteria for judgements and decisions to hand. Our judgement processes, however, often seem to run automatically, without our having constantly to explain them to ourselves.

One might suppose that, because evaluations form such an integral part of our normal routine and experience, evaluating the performance of others would not present any difficulties at all. That this is not the case has a whole host of reasons. The most important are:

- Performance evaluation does not only concern just the appraisee and employer. It has an effect, sometimes even a considerable one, on the appraisee's, i.e. the employee's, interests. This can bear on income, future work, promotion and, of course, also self-esteem, security and status.
- Whether the results are clear-cut or not, there must be feedback on performance evaluations. That means that it is often difficult both to carry out and be subject to appraisals, and can also cause problems of communication and perception.
- Evaluations take place on a level of interaction. Such interactions often demonstrate differences in power and agenda, which increases the potential for conflict.

It is therefore not surprising that everyone involved in these essential and fundamentally normal judgements and evaluations has to apply a considerable and rather complex degree of effort.

Evaluation in Business

The principles of evaluation, in terms of how they are discussed in this book, apply not only to market enterprises but to all organizations where people work together to achieve levels of performance that will bring about the desired results. These organizations may be intent on making a profit, or they may be non-profit-making organizations such as charitable institutions, hospitals, theatres, health insurance companies, interest groups, political parties or cooperatives, to name just a few.

> In every type of business and organization, evaluation is an important management tool. It has great significance for the efficiency of a business, for the utilization of available resources, for the management of business processes and finally for the very achievement of the business objectives.

At the same time evaluation is one of the basic requirements for a successful human resource policy – provided that it works. Whether or not it works, however, depends on many variables. These are mainly:

- business culture
- management style
- the form and objectives of the chosen system

- the role played by both parties in the official evaluation process
- the way in which the evaluation results are used
- the support and assistance offered by advisors and helpers.

Evaluation – by which we mean the principles governing the process as well as the evaluation system itself – is important for everyone involved as it affects very serious issues.

'Functional' 'Top-down' Evaluation

The people involved in evaluations are essentially members of an organization, regardless of their capacity or level of work. Everyone, with the exception of those 'at the very top' or 'at the very bottom', both conducts and is the subject of evaluations. This traditionally occurred in a hierarchical relationship, whereby a person reporting on a colleague conducted an evaluation, while also being subject to evaluation by someone on the immediately higher level.

> Evaluating 'from top to bottom' is a necessity that no organization or business should shy away from. The procedure is an important factor in success, both for economic efficiency and for the efficient use of human resources. Hence everything must be done to implement it as successfully as possible and to prepare everyone concerned for accomplishing this vital task.

In the following pages we will primarily discuss this typical form of performance evaluation. Since it is so crucial to business and human resource policies, this can also be considered the fundamental form of evaluation.

There are two interesting types of evaluation, which invert or modify the 'top-down' system and deserve a brief mention.

'Bottom-up' Evaluation

This does not occur very often, and only as an addition to 'top-down' evaluation.

Inverting the performer–subject relationship changes the essence, content and above all the purpose of evaluation. What is now judged is not in the first instance professional performance or the superior's contribution to the achievements of the business, but above all the way in which he or she functions as leader of a department or a team. It concerns things like communication, motivation, commitment, credibility, and training, but also efficiency, objectives, supervision and feedback.

In the main these and other factors do assess performance in terms of fulfilling objectives, but in terms of interpersonal relationships between subordinate and superior, discussing it subjectively in reports, feedback and criticism – either positively or negatively. This can readily lead to an understanding between both parties about changes in the superior's or the subordinate's behaviour.

Exactly how someone who is the subject of 'bottom-up' evaluation is treated can strongly influence how the department, group or even the entire business cooperate. The author himself experienced the following case: at the end of a discussion on evaluation the head of a department personally summarized for his workers the comments and critical issues passed on to him, and he then added his intentions and expectations of what he wanted to maintain or change.

Even more so than top-down evaluation, the inverse process is highly dependent upon the structure and culture of the group as well as the prevailing interpersonal relationships. Evaluation 'from bottom to top' should therefore not be made compulsory, because it deals with criteria that are even harder to determine than the performance objectives concerning the business as a whole. Hence the willingness and above all the ability to evaluate depends much more keenly than in a top-down exchange on the interpersonal competence of the people involved, who really need to want it to work. If evaluating 'from top to bottom' is already difficult enough, then its inverse is in some situations simply unworkable.

The '360-Degree' Evaluation

This form deviates from the vertical, hierarchical arrangement in that every member of an organization is placed at the centre point of a circle embracing all related employees, superiors and colleagues. This circle frequently extends to people who are attached to distant parts of the business, or even to members of an external organization (such as suppliers and customers), provided they are connected with a central figure and the specific work.

The subject of the evaluation, however, is not only figuratively but also literally at the centre of the evaluation process. Hence it is clear why it is called the '360-degree' evaluation. The subjects of an appraisal use their own initiative to gather 'evaluations' from the different 'evaluators' and thus form their own complete picture. It is also primarily their responsibility to draw the resulting conclusions. In general there is no reporting system to piece together the results of a 360-degree evaluation or to suggest future action, for instance in personal development or determining pay. That remains as always the remit of the functional evaluation, nor can this be replaced by the 360-degree evaluation.

The 360-degree evaluation is exclusively a private matter for each individual. It is therefore governed mainly through either an innate or a developed measure of responsibility, interest and initiative. Personality and motivation play an important role in this.

Under these circumstances, is a 'system' for the 360-degree evaluation required? Not really. There have always been people who have not used or even heard of the term '360-degree', yet behave according to its principles by looking for multiple feedback from the widest possible range of people with whom they have had contact in their private and working lives and whose opinion they value. They have always pricked up their ears so that they might pick up and heed the echo of their statements and feedback on their actions. Some people, on the other hand, are less concerned about what takes place on the outside and look more inwardly, acting in the first instance upon their own acquired or inherited principles of behaviour and way of life.

However, if the advantages gained by a 360-degree evaluation are to be made accessible to as many employees and members of the organization as possible, it is helpful to explain the principle and the most suitable way of proceeding. At the same time it can also be pointed out that the evaluation reflects a value within the framework of the business culture, and it should be made clear that the 360-degree evaluation acknowledges that initiative, openness, impartiality, responsibility and autonomy are necessary, positive and desirable. Support in answering questions and clearing up doubts is also prudent. Many people, who might at first shy away from this form of evaluation, can thus be helped to use it to their advantage.

It would, however, be counterproductive to make 360-degree evaluation obligatory for everyone. It is, even more so than bottom-up evaluation, an option that brings advantages to those who consciously choose it, but may make others feel uneasy or even do them significant harm.

> While functional evaluation is as unavoidable as day-to-day management or market research, bottom-up and 360-degree evaluations are options that people can adopt at their own discretion.

The Why and Wherefore of Functional Evaluation

At the risk of repetition, it should again be emphasized that a functional system of performance evaluation is one of the most fundamental requirements for successful business and human resource policy.

While in the past widely varying evaluation systems were often adopted for the various categories of employees and levels of hierarchy, today far-reaching differentiation seems less and less practical. It has already been emphasized how far organizations and structures have changed. We have long since discarded the once common idea of the 'unqualified' or 'unskilled' worker who could perform only simple tasks and had to be incessantly directed and monitored. There are hardly any jobs that require people without qualifications or training, at least in developed industrial and post-industrial societies.

Earlier we mentioned *Evaluating Managers' Performance* (a 1989 publication by the author). The terms used then may have been subject to a degree of change over the course of time, but they are in many respects still relevant. Individually, the terms are in general use and are not limited to what may seem a relatively small, perhaps even elitist group. The terms employee, evaluator or evaluation subject, business associate, or member of an organization no longer refer to specific levels or categories. However, terms such as superior, executive and management apply as much as ever. This is because businesses do not function as a disorderly mass; rather their members share work and distribute responsibility wherever specific aims are set.

The responsibility for managing a business lies with the executive. Indeed, in terms of a decisively and uniquely important contribution to work, executives are today found on more than just the upper levels of the hierarchy. Their duties cause them all to bear a functional responsibility. On the other hand, in terms of business law the formal – and very substantial – ultimate responsibility lies with organs of the business which have that specific purpose: managing directors, boards of directors and formal control organs (supervisory boards).

Every member of a business has a legitimate interest in the development and success of performance evaluation and, as an integral constituent of its process, is also partly responsible for it. As with all important strategic measures, the ultimate responsibility lies with the uppermost management levels; the heads of personnel, or human resource, are responsible for the technical aspect of the evaluation process.

> From the employee's point of view the evaluation process is a question of fairness and from the management's point of view it is a question of the efficient utilization of human resources.

For workers at all levels and in all categories it is important to be clear about how their performance is assessed. They can then form expectations and tackle weaknesses; they will also be better placed to decide prudently for themselves whether their particular positions, or even their fields of business, are right for them in the long term. For the supervisors and top-level management a shrewd performance evaluation system can yield vital information about the need for training, career and employment plans and, not least, provide a basis for a performance-related pay policy.

In reality the question is not whether there should be evaluation. The question is how it should be carried out. It has already been indicated that judging and evaluating is a necessity that can neither be avoided nor diminished. There is no situation in which two or more people work, live or somehow 'function' together without a 'judgement' taking place in one form or another. We 'judge' our family members, friends, colleagues, fellow employees, and superiors; we 'judge' actors, lecturers and television presenters just as we do officials, stewardesses and taxi drivers.

> Among other things, evaluation systems in businesses help to establish reasonable evaluation criteria, enable effective communication to facilitate managing the business and achieving objectives, and help to set up a system of classifying and utilizing evaluation results.
>
> Every employee has a decisive responsibility for and influence on evaluations, whether conducting them or subject to them or, as is very often the case, in both capacities.

Structure, Culture and Style

Performance evaluation is more than just a technique that can be used on any employee to draw up a current list of performance capacity and efficiency. More importantly, there is a powerful interaction between business culture, organization structure and style of evaluation. It is in this context that management and communication style play an important role.

There are many different ways to define and categorize management style and the communication style that goes with it. As this belongs only on the fringes of our study, it suffices to mention the well-known classification according to degrees of liberty. This identifies a domineering style (authoritarian, patriarchal); a style of provision and imposition (paternalistic); a style based on listening and partnership (participatory); and styles based on consensus.

There is also a variety of definitions and categorizations for business or organization culture. Wendy Hall has put forward one interesting analysis (*Managing Cultures: Making Strategic Alliances Work*), whereby she describes different forms of business culture in terms of three main criteria:

- *Artefacts and etiquette:* This refers to how people greet one another, inner architecture, clothing, use of first or surnames.
- *Behaviours and actions:* For example the way conflicts are resolved, use of gestures and symbols, use of language.
- *Core morals, beliefs, values:* This mainly refers to outside influences such as religious traditions, the way people are traditionally brought up, legal norms and so on.

Hall suggests that different organization cultures emerge depending on the type and intensity of the effect that these crucial influences have. The different cultures reflect both characteristics generated and evolved from within (criteria 1 and 2), and cultural influences of the environment on a national and ethical scale (criterion 3).

In the same way that a business is departmentalized, that responsibility is shared, or that official channels of control are set up, so organizational structure depends upon the degree of centralization or decentralization in terms of distributing work and responsibility. Organizational structure is a result of amalgamations of objectives and control, and may thus take various forms: functional, profit-centre, divisional, multi-dimensional (matrix) or even project structure. The author of this book has written more about organizational structure in *Personnel Management in the New Europe*.

It is clear that an authoritarian, centralist style in management, communication, culture and structure offers completely different conditions for evaluation than a style based on consensus in a multi-dimensional structure where there is extensive delegation. On the other hand, however, the mere existence of evaluation will influence whatever business culture and management style is in place. Furthermore, it is wholly legitimate to influence management style purposefully through a specific evaluation plan, provided that this takes place with full awareness, agreement and specific aims, and without a 'hidden agenda'.

It is fair to conclude that there is no single answer to the question of which is the most suitable evaluation system. It is more appropriate to ask whether a system should be made to adjust to a certain style or whether it should shape it. If by introducing or renewing an evaluation system the intention is to make a strongly paternalistic management style more inclusive, then it is critical that the executives and above all the senior managers identify with this objective completely. Otherwise the experiment would be doomed from the outset. Should evaluation be made subordinate to an existing business culture, then that must also be clarified from the very start in order to avoid misunderstanding and disappointment.

Perception

Before we consider a series of variations and forms of performance evaluation, it is necessary to refer to one of the most significant variables of the entire question: subjective perception.

We aim to evaluate on the most factual, intelligible and concrete basis possible, especially when evaluating work performance. Objectivity should lend credibility to the whole process, put the results beyond dispute and thereby appeal to reason when consequences have to be drawn from such a coordinated evaluation.

We all know from experience that there are limits to this. Perceptions, impressions and interpretations even of apparently incontrovertible facts can vary greatly from person to person. Moreover, a certain degree of opportunism or a need for justification and self-confirmation can play a part. The author was well acquainted with one leading manager of a large business who used to say '*En cas d'echec les faits ont tort*' (In case of failure the facts are wrong). But there is more than this.

Objectivity seems to be a goal that can only be approached as an asymptote: it can never be reached completely

C. G. Jung described an individual's forms of perception and evaluation as that person's own cognitive style, which determines how information is analysed. This analysis provides the framework for a judgement, thus leading to an evaluation. According to this, there are two dimensions to perception. The first is sensory perception: becoming aware of hard facts. The other is intuitive perception: meanings and possibilities beyond conscious perception. Sensory perception gives rise to 'analytical' evaluation, while intuitive perception generates 'emotional' evaluation.

Without dwelling on Jung we can claim that 'facts' are never merely 'facts' and that between sensory and intuitive perception there are huge individual differences. In just the same way there will also be an immense variation in the degree of analytical application and emotional influence. There can be little faith in so-called objective facts. What might be for one person a march of extreme right-wing demonstrators is for another the procession of a quaint rifle club.

Merely retaining a share of the market might for one person be a tremendous achievement, unparalleled in the face of competitors' cut-throat price policies, but in the eyes of another it is a failure, for the predicted growth and the targets set to achieve it have not been delivered. Analytical evaluation is simple and clear: the share of the market was X and remains so. In the first person's view, the emotional component argues: 'if we had not . . . then the share of the market would have diminished and this could have surprised nobody'. The intuitive perception and emotional evaluation of the second person, however, assert 'there is always one reason or another why it does not work, but the trick is to find a new way so that the goal can indeed be reached'.

In a very detailed scientific examination of 'the meaning of perception in personnel assessment' Günter Lueger argued:

> Judgements in personnel assessment are not isomorphic reproductions of the performance-related behaviour of the organization member who is being appraised, but are distorted through a multitude of factors that influence perception processes. The way evaluation systems are devised might reduce distortions of perception, but cannot prevent them.
>
> (Lueger, 1993)

As well as deficiencies in perception, Lueger's analysis also identifies misinterpretations that may arise out of failures in evaluation, inherent aberrations of behaviour and a whole host of empirically established tendencies in forming judgements, which influence evaluation results. Some examples of these are:

- The *Halo effect*: this entails a particularly strongly positive characteristic dominating the others.
- The *attribution mistake:* this arises when the person evaluating a specific achievement (or lack of achievement) puts it down to causes other than the true ones. This is similar to the *fundamental attribution error* described in the early 1980s by Peters and Waterman in their cult book on management *In Search of Excellence*. They exposed the tendency to ascribe every success to 'ourselves' but every shortcoming to 'the others'.
- The author has at times observed what he calls the *lion effect* after the verb 'to lionize' (treating someone as a celebrity). After a series of successes, failures no longer count because heroes always win and the lion is always the King of the Beasts.
- There is a common tendency, in self-evaluation, for people to demand too much of themselves when predetermined evaluation scales are in place. This can readily be understood as a distortion of perception. It certainly seems that when scales are used, analytical evaluation (which expects a statistically sound spread of results) is overruled by emotional evaluation. This can easily be put to the test. At least 90 per cent of people in every group, whether they are participants in a meeting, students in a lecture theatre, members of a club or even the employees of a firm, will respond positively when asked if they see themselves as above average. From a detached and analytical perspective we might conclude that the figure cannot be more than 50 per cent statistically speaking, but in specific and above all personal terms this conclusion is intuitively rejected.
- The phenomenon of *selective communication or perception* is also often apparent. People give only as much information as they want to reveal, not everything they should. By the same token people hear only what they want to hear, blocking out unwelcome news.

These and other phenomena will be discussed in detail in the section that examines resolving problems and overcoming difficulties.

Features of Performance Evaluation

Evaluations can, independent of the particular system, either be furnished with certain features or properties or develop these themselves as they are implemented.

Informal or Institutionalized

There is a fundamental difference between *informal* and *institutionalized evaluation*. As we have claimed and hopefully demonstrated, evaluation goes on at all times and in all places. Perhaps there are no universally certified principles of evaluation and there may be no formal evaluation system, but there are at least judgements, both analytical and intuitive. They may not be visible and may remain unexpressed – except perhaps indirectly – but they are always there, in the minds of those who have made them. By their nature such judgements remain obscure.

If performance evaluation is run according to principles, procedures and systems, it is institutionalized and is thus more transparent, intelligible and easier to review, and can serve more diverse purposes, which we will discuss later.

Open or Secret

This phrase, suggesting as it does the possibility of a more or less secret evaluation, may come as a surprise. The reality, however, is that there have been such outwardly patriarchal practices, and perhaps they still exist in pockets here and there.

For many reasons, including legal regulations governing industrial relations, it is hard to imagine that a 'secret' evaluation system would be introduced anywhere today. There are nevertheless existing practices that leave a lot to be desired in terms of transparency.

Disadvantages: A drawback to secrecy is that it vitiates almost all of the beneficial effects that both the business and employee would otherwise experience, quite apart from any damage that might be done to management style, credibility, trust and business culture. It is occasionally argued that confidentiality is the only way to guarantee evaluation procedures, but this argument is not very convincing or forward-looking.

Character-based

The criteria for this form of performance evaluation are qualities and characteristics that are vital for efficiency and success in a particular job, or even in a particular organization. Character appraisals therefore build upon the individual profile of performance requirements. The appraisal takes account of personality traits such as creativity, ability to withstand stress, good nature, loyalty, ambition, intelligence, perhaps humour too and similar characteristics.

Advantages: Appraisals based on personality are desirable when a causal relationship between performance and individual traits can be traced. Substantial appraisals that measure performance quantitatively or qualitatively might be impractical, or only possible in the long term. In such cases it may be expedient to evaluate according to effort rather than results, as achievements might not yet be available or conducive to evaluation. This process assumes that if the requirements are met and the effort put in, then the result will also be acceptable. This may be entirely appropriate in certain fields, such as in research, in academia, and perhaps also in personnel management.

Disadvantages: The dangers of overcooked character appraisals lie in the ambiguity of the terms employed. (Even the everyday word 'intelligence' proves under closer scrutiny to be extremely cryptic: does it refer to creative, practical, or emotional intelligence; and even if it can be defined, are these definitions then sufficiently clear?) It can also lead to the excessive practice of amateur psychology. All in all, character appraisals encourage a high degree of subjectivity.

Task-based

The properties of this evaluation focus not so much on the person but on the content of the task to be carried out. The fundamental assumption here is that in every job there are certain essential tasks that have a decisive impact on success or failure. Therefore the evaluation is devised to monitor quite precisely the specifications of the task (which of course must then actually be assigned). Miscellaneous individual details are either not mentioned at all if they are irrelevant to this, or mentioned only when they positively or negatively influence the fulfilment, the performance, of the task.

Advantages: Compared to character appraisals this form of evaluation has the advantage of greater substance and objectivity. It is best implemented where the parameters in which the task is carried out are stable over a long period of time, or where stability and constancy form a fundamental part of fulfilling the task. This is, for example, appropriate for sections of public administration or in the long-term planning and coordination of large businesses. As it is rather inflexible, this form of evaluation makes it necessary to adjust task specifications regularly to new demands.

Disadvantages: A further aspect that can be viewed as a disadvantage is that the aforementioned interrelation with task specifications can be extremely limiting and bureaucratic, especially when this causes delays or difficulties in implementing alterations.

Target-based

This basically takes task-based methods a stage further. In an ever more dynamically changing world, businesses and the people who work in them must adapt extremely quickly to new challenges, grasping new opportunities as positions at work and the content of jobs change frequently and radically. This means that task specifications do not provide a flexible enough basis for performance evaluation, since they would increasingly evaluate people according to criteria that are no longer relevant or that have been displaced.

In general target-based evaluation assumes that in every task and for every worker we can define a number of main aims (realistically at the most five, better no more than three) that impact on success or failure. These aims are predetermined at least a year in advance: in the main they stem logically from the annual plan. Individual (or group) performance is measured against the achievement of these aims.

Target-based performance evaluation is a variation of 'Management by Objectives' (see pages 34–7), albeit generally a little less all-embracing, thus lending to its processes a strongly operational and consciously unbureaucratic character. It is by nature best placed wherever the main strategic emphases change frequently, which is indeed happening everywhere to a growing extent.

It is vital that the emphasis on setting and achieving targets primarily assesses the result and not the effort.

Result-based

When numerous unpredictable variables make formal target setting impracticable, then there can, or rather must, be an evaluation of the objectives actually attained as well as an appraisal of the performance put in to achieve those results.

To do this, it can sometimes help to make comparisons and analogies. Thus branches compare themselves against one another, while large businesses look to recognized analyses of the economic press, such as *Fortune 500* or the *Financial Times 100*, to compare their results with businesses in the same 'peer group'. Of course only the largest (and therefore not very many) businesses qualify for this type of comparison.

An effective way to relativize results is to compare over a period of time within the same firm. In this way a series of years are called up and – as far as it is possible and appropriate – the irregularities that have caused the peaks or troughs are erased. This then creates a good basis for comparison, from which it can be inferred whether result X is good, bad or average.

Advantages: Target-based and result-based methods are increasingly employed because they are inherently very flexible and are strategically relevant, which affords them a high degree of objectivity.

Disadvantages: Both methods also have disadvantages. It is important to be aware that concentrating on business objectives and results makes it harder to pay attention to individual highs and lows. Also, there needs to be constant critical examination of the quality of the objectives and the interpretation of the results.

In contrast to strictly quantitative results (or even objectives), it is harder to make good use of those that can only be measured or defined qualitatively. But to evaluate exclusively in quantitative terms because of this – because it makes measurement easier – would certainly be damaging in the long term, for it could distort priorities and trivialize the evaluation.

Aims of Performance Evaluation

As we have seen, the various types of performance evaluation work towards different aims. It is therefore worthwhile to consider exactly which of the different varieties should be selected, or alternatively to look for a pragmatic blend that aligns the crucial business issues with the chief aims of evaluations.

Character appraisals and *task-based evaluations* set out mainly to record long-term performance ability and can therefore also yield information about an employee's potential and development possibilities. In terms of wage policy they influence advancement only within a predetermined framework or guideline.

Result or *target-based evaluations* set out primarily to record short-term performance efficiency and therefore are significant predominantly for reward policies, especially in the context of bonuses or other incentive systems.

In each example it is vital that evaluation is based on a continuous process. This means that evaluation represents substantially more than filling out forms once a year. Evaluation is among other things a tool of management and as such has a lot to do with communication, motivation and feedback.

The evaluation cycle thus begins by establishing and agreeing upon objectives or key issues for the coming business period, during which there should be an occasional mutual check of progress. It is vitally important to identify and discuss positives and negatives at the earliest opportunity. It would be less constructive to wait until the annual evaluation review. Furthermore, this review should in principle provide more an opportunity to summarize mutually and to examine the period of performance that has elapsed than to weigh good points against bad. It should therefore in general also throw up no great surprises for both evaluator and the subject of the evaluation.

Basically, performance evaluations set out to draw a line under performance levels or achievements.

At the same time evaluation also means differentiation. On the one hand this is based on the knowledge that different people produce varying levels of performances, and on the other hand there is the necessity to highlight these differences and to make use of them. This can be achieved, for example, in personal development or in determining wages. If such objectives are irrelevant, then a formalised evaluation is not necessary: it takes place informally anyway, as was mentioned at the very start.

Differentiation accords with our sense of fairness. Performance should be a yardstick for pay and promotion. At the same time differentiation also provides fuel for conflict. While most people, at least in Western cultures, agree with the principle of 'meritocracy', in practice and in terms of its effect at the level of the individuals concerned, a discrepancy in this principle is sometimes felt. Eastern cultures, such as Japan, Indonesia and Thailand, are more inclined to withdraw from differentiation, especially when it is openly declared. Evaluation systems resembling our models are also much less likely to be found there. In traditionally run businesses in the East, evaluation is rather more covert. It is true that Western influence, particularly in subsidiaries of Western businesses, is really quite considerable, but this still does not guarantee cultural acceptance of Western principles.

The main objectives of institutionalized evaluation systems, which aim not only to assess, but also to innovate, motivate and differentiate, lie in the following areas:

- reward policy
- definition of training needs
- career and employment plans
- performance incentives
- elimination of weaknesses
- more targeted leadership
- emphasizing strategic key issues
- more efficient communication.

As with all methods and processes, performance evaluation can achieve its aims fully, partially or not at all. Apart from the fact that the method of evaluating should be reasonable, it is critically important for success that the uppermost heads of management not only support the principle of evaluation but also practise it.

The elements forming the basis of evaluation consist of:

Objective → Performance → Evaluation → Feedback → New objective

Filling out formulas and lists for purely administrative purposes does not suffice here. Of critical significance is how evaluations form an integral part of the strategic planning and control processes of the business.

We will later discuss the most important factors of success and thereby also examine how to resolve problems and overcome difficulties.

The Evaluation Review

The evaluation review is an integral part of the evaluation process. It simplifies an overview of what has been achieved, offers the possibility for critical reassessment, makes feedback possible and prepares the way for measures designed to build on strengths and eradicate weaknesses.

The evaluation review should not be a dramatic climax, but the logical conclusion and overview of an evaluation period, perhaps of one business year. It is also the evidence and touchstone for determining whether communication and feedback have functioned between superior and employee.

If all goes well the evaluation review should not bring any surprises for either party, but afford a constructive opportunity to discuss strengths and weaknesses as well as helpful and inhibiting factors. At the same time it provides the foundation for new objectives and performance enhancing measures. The evaluation review can be an extremely motivating experience for both the performer and the subject of evaluation.

PREPARING FOR THE REVIEW

- Evaluators have a duty to ensure that the evaluation they carry out is precisely and completely recorded in writing. A formula is normally used for this.
- They should be clear about what the evaluation review is meant to achieve.
- It is good to give an account of what people being evaluated have achieved and the conditions which helped or perhaps hindered them.
- Evaluators should again go over the relevant crucial points and specific intentions that were brought up and discussed during the evaluation period.
- Evaluators should empathize with the people being evaluated and try to anticipate what their views and expectations could be.
- Inventing a certain 'style' for the review that is otherwise alien to the evaluator should be avoided for several reasons. First, it is usually very hard to maintain over a long period, second it generally makes the evaluator appear artificial, and finally the review should as far as possible seem no different from any normal day of working together.
- It is very important that all foreseeable disruptions are eliminated for the duration of the review.
- Both evaluator and the subject of the evaluation (who should prepare for the review in a similar way to the evaluator) should agree upon a mutually convenient date for this review.

THE REVIEW ITSELF

The evaluation review should be a mutual undertaking to which both the evaluator and the subject of evaluation contribute accordingly.

Even with the best preparation, the degree of openness and courage needed for successful evaluation review should not be underestimated. It was not without reason that one large business opted for 'Honesty and Courage' as the maxim for its established evaluation system. Demands for honesty and courage may well have been somewhat more difficult to fulfil in 'hierarchical' times than in a 'post-hierarchical' era of more open, uncomplicated communication, yet experience demonstrates that they are still far from a matter of course. Most people evidently find it easier to put their thoughts in clear and unmistakeable words on paper than to tell someone face to face. There is often an understandable desire to avoid potential conflicts right at the very start. Thus if a written report is available it is worth letting the subject of the evaluation read it before the review, and if need be warn them in advance that perhaps not everything in it will beget unmitigated joy or agreement.

It will often be found that the evaluation review cannot be completed in one single meeting. Because pressure of time is not conducive to the quality of the review, and especially if a problem comes to light that needs a constructive examination of all its aspects, it might be preferable to continue the review on another day. This also gives both parties time for contemplation.

In general, evaluation is not only the responsibility of the immediate supervisor; the superior one further step up the ladder also has a certain role to play. Thus before the review the evaluator should have coordinated the evaluation with the higher levels. Possible 'evaluation processes' should be clear to all parties in advance.

Here a few more simple *directions for conducting the review:*

- Above all, evaluators should make clear their role, their duties and the results they are expecting and aiming for. Comments about the subject's person or character are seldom useful or professionally necessary. Evaluators should be prepared to listen and to really address the issues of the evaluation subject. They should, however, only alter their initial standpoint when they are convinced, not when they are coaxed, or when facts rather than emotions require it.
- Discussion of the achievements of other employees should be avoided. Such comparisons do not normally lead very far and often result in emotional judgements prevailing over analytical ones.
- Ideally the evaluation review should be held sufficiently far from payday to avoid talk of previous or forthcoming wage increases or bonus payments. The opposite might seem truer to some, who feel that in a system that assesses performance, evaluation reviews bear directly on payment and performance. Experience shows, however, that when evaluations and reviews coincide with releasing information about wage alterations, bonuses and suchlike, these matters force the real issues of the review to the sidelines. There is a lot to be said against discussing too many issues in a single review. The evaluation itself already embraces so many serious points that it demands complete attention, as the real-life example illustrates (see Chapter 4).
- When the evaluation and review have been concluded, it is generally not necessary later to explain in detail the basis on which an employee has been paid. This is generally evident – or at least should be – and hides no more major surprises.

The person being evaluated should attempt to explain impartially any disruptive factors that they are aware of. They should be prepared to suggest ways for improvement. They should have considered what further training might be beneficial. It should be remembered that businesses are not obliged to provide training to the employee. Individual responsibility and initiative are vital, especially in view of the fact that training and further development are crucial if knowledge, experience and skills are to be kept right up to date.

In general there is just as much onus on the subject of an evaluation as there is on the evaluator to gain as much as they possibly can from the process. To do this, questions concerning both the internal and external workings of the organization, processes, communication, efficiency and operation (competitors, customer orientations, public relations and suchlike) must be critically examined.

The Working Relationship

Most people value harmonious and carefree relationships with one another. The relationship between superior and subordinate is no exception. Great value is rightly placed on healthy cooperation, and in general effort is taken not to damage the atmosphere with negativity. To preclude unnecessary emotions, worries arising out of daily duties, tensions, deadline pressures and many other factors are kept largely on a professional and rational level, without personal undertones.

An open and honest evaluation will normally contain criticism, too; sometimes there will be a lot to find fault with. That can be experienced negatively by the employee and lead to frustration and other undesirable reactions. This can damage cooperation and, in particular, performance. The exact opposite of what the evaluation actually intended will then be achieved: a negative instead of a constructive atmosphere, and poorer performance and results instead of improvement.

There is therefore sometimes a (completely understandable) tendency to avoid this type of disruptive influence, so that evaluations overemphasize all of the positive aspects and underplay or entirely omit the negative ones. Furthermore, it can often be easier to have recourse to the 'system', the 'bureaucracy' or the next level in the hierarchy in order to take the edge out of a not entirely positive evaluation and thereby try to avoid a possible deterioration of the working relationship. Shortcomings are also often seen as unchangeable, and there may be a desire to avoid mentioning them in an evaluation review for fear of sullying the atmosphere or destroying illusions.

All of this can be improved by treating evaluation as a continuous process and by the superior ensuring that the employee is constantly given feedback over success and failure, over good and bad performance. Additionally, an effort should be made to instil the belief in everybody involved that the actual purpose of evaluating is to improve performance and that this is only possible when mistakes can be openly discussed. It is certainly vital that there is also real willingness to set about correcting them. This applies to the superior just as it does to the employees and the entire management team.

Selective Communication and Perception

This phrase may perhaps sound a little pompous, but it actually describes a phenomenon that is neither uncommon nor restricted to evaluations.

When someone is talking to us about ourselves, we have a predilection to hear all the nice things clearly, but hardly to hear the negative comments at all. In any case our memories retain only the positive aspects. This can be exemplified through the desire to avoid conflict that was mentioned earlier, whereby not only does hearing become selective, but even our entire means of communication. This very often occurs quite unintentionally. Many superiors are convinced that they have told their subordinates everything about their weaknesses. The employees on the other hand are firm in the belief that they have done everything to the superior's complete satisfaction.

Selection does not only take place by suppressing the negative, although this is the most common form. There is also the form that emphasizes the negative at the cost of the positive. Some people believe that praise gives rise to vanity and smugness; others consider themselves beyond compare, far excelling everyone else; yet others are insecure and dread competition, and therefore shy away from recognizing the good performance or development potential of others, including their own colleagues.

Furthermore, people who have been evaluated can sometimes obscure their positive aspects: for instance when they strongly doubt their own qualities, when they are afraid of failure or of their superior.

> Whatever form the selection of information or perception may take, each time it happens reality grows more obscure, which significantly thwarts the purpose of evaluations.

The evaluation review report drafted by both the evaluator and the evaluation subject is therefore very valuable. These reports should contain a brief summary of the main points of the review and, if applicable, the steps that have been discussed or planned. While the report should take stock of the thoughts of both parties, due care should be taken that one does not influence the report of the other. Although a bland evaluation review will not be made more meaningful simply by being written up, at least the statements that people believe they have already expressed clearly enough will be reinforced on paper and emphasized, thereby precluding the potential selection of information or perception.

The Evaluation Scale

In terms of evaluation principles and systems, emphasizing or ranking general or even specific performance areas by using a scale (e.g. 1–5) or set phrases (e.g. *Excellent* to *Unsatisfactory*) is by no means essential for a sensible evaluation system. Describing performance clearly might also suffice to work out strengths and weaknesses, and it might be possible to base various evaluation objectives on these descriptions.

In practice, however, assessments based on set phrases prove largely unavoidable. This is mainly because it is otherwise very difficult to take performance levels into account when differentiating for pay and career development. Particularly in larger businesses with many employees, 'administrative' reasons alone necessitate code and standardization. Most commonly, as mentioned above, terms such as *exceptional, very good, good, below average, unsatisfactory* are used, or letters or numbers that more or less describe the same gradations. There are systems with ten classifications, with five, with six, with three.

> Whatever form an evaluation scale takes, certain fundamental problems will always crop up when it is used. The fact that in the main too many 'good' and too few 'bad' references arise is well known. There is thus too little differentiation, as there are too few entries on the lower scale. If it is not possible to achieve a realistic measure of differentiation, then eventually and inevitably the evaluation system will not serve its purpose.

Supporters of differentiation point to many valid arguments. They refer to statistical standard distribution (the famous Gauss curve), probability, insights gained from evolution and anthropology theories, learning curves and a lot more besides. They cite the dangers of standardization, which would put the credibility of a performance-based personnel policy at stake.

The difficulty is that in principle hardly anyone is against differentiation. Only when the effects are personally felt, affecting self-evaluation and informal evaluation of one's peers, does rationality give way to emotion and analysis to intuition. This plainly and simply touches upon the human dilemma that, as already mentioned elsewhere, the massively overwhelming majority of people believe themselves to be above average. This is true of almost 100 per cent of the optimistic, ambitious and well-qualified employees of a business, among whom discriminating criteria must determine selection and development.

Attempting to resolve the problem of differentiation in evaluation simply by a ranking system will succumb to exactly the same dilemma. While everyone would rationally agree that there is a best and a worst and many shades in between, the actual consequences of such ranking are much less agreeable.

A realistic viewpoint is that an 'evaluation mark' only makes sense when it can differentiate effectively, for example in determining wages. Even then, the approach requires a constant determination to struggle against tendencies in the evaluation process that impede differentiation.

When, however, 'marks' have no real purpose, it is much better to do without them altogether. This will not compromise the legitimacy of the evaluation, but rather reinforce it. Furthermore a great deal of effort will be saved and many conflicts avoided.

The Role of the Immediately Higher Management Level

Important as the function of the higher management levels is, it is equally vital that this function is exercised with caution. It should avoid dealing with details that only the individual's immediate superior can reliably attend to. When, however, the performance level of the individual is to be compared on a broader basis and evaluations or statements about further performance potential are to be made, then insights and evaluation criteria come into play of which the immediate superior often has only limited awareness. If an evaluation carried out by the immediate superior is to be altered, then this should happen only with agreement and consultation.

It is also very important to follow the correct procedures carefully. Hence it is unwise to conduct evaluation reviews before the evaluation has run through the 'official channels'. It is always simpler and more practicable first to propose alterations in evaluations (such as those occasioned by new factors emerging from conversations with the evaluation subject) to a superior further up the chain of command than initially to revise the evaluation, only to have to modify the results later.

Comparisons between Business Areas

Some evaluators are known to be 'generous', others to be 'mean'. It may be easier to shine in some areas than in others.

It is of course not always possible to tell a justified evaluation from an unjustified one. Two measures above all could help to ward against standardization on the one hand and discrimination on the other: the first is to train all evaluators intensively, and the second is to harmonize all evaluation results between the different departments and business areas. The latter is again primarily the task of the higher management levels; those responsible in the personnel department should also assist.

Bureaucracy

While it is necessary to have a degree of consistency regarding the content of the evaluation, procedures and schedules, there is always a certain danger of overdoing formulas and reports. There are many separate steps involved, from job descriptions through to setting targets, adjusting targets to new circumstances, comparing targets with the actual results, evaluating, checking with higher levels, reporting on evaluation reviews and the like, and on to setting new targets. Each step, however, should be free from the need to deploy an array of potentially extensive bureaucratic measures.

> More than a few evaluation systems have ultimately failed because they were no longer practically manageable since they no longer accorded to normal standards of efficiency.

Unfortunately many system developers overlook the fact that most system users are frightened off by too much attention to detail and procedural complexity. If systems require intense commitments of time and effort, the conflicts with other priorities become too great.

Fairness and Objectivity

Understandably, questions about fairness and objectivity will invariably be posed and, just as regularly, there will be no completely satisfactory answers.

Evaluation both as a principle and as a process is in itself highly subjective, because in essence it is based on how the subjects of evaluations see themselves and how the evaluator sees them. The mutual assessments that subject and evaluator make of each other adds a further subjective variable, so much so that subjectivity almost knows no bounds.

Thus we can speak only of *relative objectivity*. This can be reinforced, mainly through procedures and good training of the evaluator, but also by evaluation subjects thoroughly informing themselves about the essence and intention of the evaluation. Choosing a suitable format, objective and criteria is therefore of vital importance.

Possibilities of Appeal

The subjects of evaluations should not have the impression that they are at the mercy of the evaluator for better or worse.

There can well be a difference of opinion so serious that the people involved cannot resolve it. It would be wrong to let this damage the entire working relationship for a lengthy period. Hence it is advisable to arrange for an escape hatch in the form of an appeals process.

This should be set up in such a way that professional resolutions are found rather than political compromises. It is therefore better to steer clear of 'arbitration commissions'. It generally suffices to give the subject of an evaluation access to the next higher superior. In most cases it is also worthwhile to draw in the personnel manager. The main task of the people concerned with the 'appeal' will be to shed light on the professional background of the evaluation and to neutralize the emotional factors that generally exist in such cases. They should therefore find out the tasks that people had, the priorities, objectives and the results actually achieved. It should come as no surprise, however, when it occasionally transpires that the actual cause of the conflict does not primarily concern the evaluation itself, but other factors.

Evaluation Routine

It is definitely not necessary to evaluate every employee every year according to every rule of the system. Such pointless bureaucracy would be more likely to damage the credibility and efficacy of the evaluation procedure than benefit it.

The rules allowing for deviations from evaluation should obviously be very clear. Evaluations will generally be deemed unnecessary if someone has already carried out the same work for a long time (although conversely, especially in more highly qualified and management positions, formal evaluations are hardly sensible after less than one year), if someone only has a few years left until retirement, if the evaluator and evaluation subject have already worked together in the same capacity for a very long time, and in similar circumstances.

Participation, File Access, Data Protection

It need hardly be emphasized that all cases must take account of and comply with the letter and spirit of relevant legal requirements. To examine the legal aspects in detail would stray too far away from the present theme. Any regulatory regime will normally be designed in a way that is not incompatible with a sensible evaluation policy. In any case it is basically true that the efforts and exertions of the evaluation process are only worthwhile when there is enough freedom for movement to allow legitimate goals to be both aspired to and achieved in the interests of the business, its management and their employees.

Developing and Applying the System

There is a certain potential for conflict between those who 'create' or develop an evaluation system (perhaps the personnel manager or business advisor) and the 'users' (meaning the other managers and employees in the business).

One of the fundamental tasks of the personnel manager and the relevant experts is, of course, to create concepts, systems and methods that conform to every rule in the book and are thus 'state of the art'. The origins of errors and weaknesses in these systems often seem in practice impossible to root out. However they can often be traced, among other causes, to a series of misunderstandings, lack of time or lack of interest, but above all to the system developers treating the system users like children. In extreme cases this leads to general mutual animosity, mistrust and indignation.

It is true to say of evaluation methods therefore – as of many other practices too – that they fail when they:

- are imposed from the outside or from above
- are alien to the objectives
- are suspected of being manipulative
- are complicated and costly to implement.

Conversely, they have more chance of success when they:

- are integrated in the management and business objectives
- help to achieve these objectives
- and can be implemented easily and economically.

Instead of a Summary

Six Steps towards Efficient Evaluation

1. Keep all relevant documents together:
   - job description, specific tasks, projects
   - personal objectives
   - previous evaluation
   - others' opinions
   - how the evaluation was devised.

2. Be clear about the evaluation review:
   - agree a convenient time in advance
   - avoid time pressures, allow sufficient time
   - pay is a different theme altogether.

3. Objectivity:
   - remain specific and factual
   - discuss points which can be worked upon
   - avoid discussion of personality and character.

4. Do not avoid problems:
   - conduct an open discussion
   - do not sweep criticism under the carpet.

5. Agree on conclusions and actions.

6. Written summary of the review and the results.

Amusing Aside: Quotations from Evaluations

An American colleague supplied the author with the following list of
quotations from evaluations. They were handed out to the participants

during a discussion at the University of Michigan for a little entertainment. They are allegedly all authentic.

This individual has talents but has kept them well hidden.

Combs his hair to one side and appears rustic.

A quiet, reticent, neat-appearing individual – industrious, tenacious, diffident, careful and neat. I do not wish to have this person as a member of my staff at this time.

His leadership is outstanding except for his lack of ability to get on with his subordinates.

He hasn't any mental traits.

He needs careful watching since he borders on brilliant.

Believes sincerely in the power of prayer and it is astonishing to note how many times his prayers are answered.

Never makes the same mistake twice, but it seems to me that he has made them all once.

Gives the appearance of being fat due to the tight clothes he wears.

Is keenly analytical and his highly developed mentality could best be used in the research and development field. He lacks Common Sense.

An independent thinker with a mediocre mentality.

Recently married and devotes more time to this activity than to his current assignment.

Tends to create the impression of unpositive personality through needless and undiscerning gentility and softspokenness.

Of average intelligence except for lack of judgement on one occasion in attempting to capture a rattlesnake for which he was hospitalised.

The author would like to thank an English colleague for the following overview of evaluation criteria and their definitions. These notes are allegedly not authentic and also not entirely without irony.

Guide to Managers' and Subordinates' Performance Review

Definition of Performance:

1 = Far exceeds job requirements
2 = Exceeds job requirements
3 = Meets job requirements
4 = Needs some improvement
5 = Does not meet minimum requirements

Evaluation Criteria:

EFFECTIVENESS:
1 = Leaps tall buildings with a single bound
2 = Must take a running start to leap over tall buildings
3 = Can only leap over a short building or medium building with no spires
4 = Crashes into buildings when attempting to jump over them
5 = Cannot recognize buildings at all, let alone jump over them

SPEED OF WORKING:
1 = Is faster than a speeding bullet
2 = Is as fast as a speeding bullet
3 = Not quite as fast
4 = Would you believe a slow bullet?
5 = Wounds self with bullets when attempting to shoot gun

ENERGY:
1 = Is stronger than a locomotive
2 = Is stronger than a bull elephant
3 = Is stronger than a bull
4 = Shoots the bull
5 = Smells like a bull

ADAPTABILITY:

1 = Walks on water consistently
2 = Walks on water in emergencies
3 = Washes with water
4 = Drinks water
5 = Passes water

COMMUNICATION:

1 = Talks with God
2 = Talks with angels
3 = Talks to himself
4 = Argues with himself
5 = Loses those arguments

CHAPTER 3

Evaluation of Potential

Performance and Potential are not Identical

What is achieved today does not reliably indicate what can be achieved tomorrow. A business which has delivered growth and profit today or over the last 10 or 15 years might be able to do the same in the future but there are no absolute guarantees. The question is whether it has the potential to do so.

> It is extremely positive and deserving of reward when an employee fulfils a task exceptionally well. But to conclude immediately from this that other tasks can be mastered just as proficiently may be a losing gamble.

It has long been known that achievements in school and higher education cannot reliably gauge future career success and the ability to cope with life. Generations of failing pupils and their parents have consoled themselves with the fact that giants such as Churchill and Einstein – allegedly – had only mediocre success at school. This is not to suggest an inverse correlation between school success and later career, but if the selection of employees boiled down exclusively to the school report, then errors of selection would invariably be pre-programmed.

It would be just as flawed to make selections by taking any other single criterion as the singularly decisive factor, whether it be sex, political orientation, social status, linguistic skill, knowledge of foreign languages, club membership, contacts or any one of a host of other possibilities. Furthermore, reliance solely upon methods such as specific tests, handwriting analyses or astrological findings carries a danger of neglecting crucial points that these cannot identify. (It is not the purpose here to discuss what information might be gleaned from particular tests, or whether graphology or astrology might afford practical insights, as this would stray too far from the subject.)

> Quite apart from the fact that omitting certain details can have a discriminating effect, it is simply and plainly misleading to try to infer from one single trait an assessment of ability, and above all an evaluation of future performance capacity and development potential. This does not mean that the individual criterion is necessarily irrelevant, but it acts in combination with a host of others, and so has only relative significance.

It has happened, and still happens all too often, that a line is drawn from today's performance into the future and it is assumed that the capacity to fulfil higher tasks successfully can be deduced from this. Observing the negative consequences of this practice, however, has led to the formulation of the well-known 'Peter Principle': everybody is promoted until they reach a 'level of incompetence'. This – somewhat exaggerated – inevitability arises from the simple assumption that 'someone who does this job well will also do the job on the next level well', and this is sustained until the promoted role is simply too much for the person to handle. It is too late then to avoid damaging the person and the business, and often too late to repair the damage.

Selection Criteria

Everywhere – or at least almost everywhere – it is the norm when choosing employees to assess a number of criteria that reflect the specific requirements of the business or organization and, by building up a picture, to decide whether or not to proceed with the appointment. The question here is not whether these selection criteria are in fact always ideal. It is the author's experience, however, that most businesses with a structured and systematic selection procedure are able to achieve a healthy strike rate. They thus have a considerable advantage over businesses that proceed arbitrarily, opportunistically or otherwise aimlessly.

Even with the best selection methods a certain number of blunders must be expected when choosing among external candidates for a job or career, for nobody really 'knows' the candidates well at all. It is likely, on the other hand, that the soundness of decisions concerning promotions from among the business's own employees should be, if not 100 per cent, then certainly very close to it. After all we are not dealing here with strangers.

In the past this lured people into inferring future potential from tasks fulfilled today, in the hope that poor decisions could be avoided as far as possible. This hope, however, was by no means always realized (see 'the

Peter Principle'). It hence became necessary to look for ways in which decisions concerning promotion and personnel development could be underpinned as firmly as possible, because good performance (although never irrelevant) did not inevitably indicate high potential. We will later discuss different variations that were developed to improve the 'predictability' of development capacity.

Because thoughtless application of 'techniques' hardly promises intelligent outcomes in terms of assessing potential or other qualities, it is desirable first to consider some fundamental points.

What is Potential?

As the capacity and ability for further development, potential is fundamentally not something that is 'created', and in essence it is not specifically to do with people in the working world more than with any others. Potential is unique to each individual, regardless of the phase of life, external conditions or the inner state of mind people find themselves in. Everybody possesses abilities and capacities, which may or may not be used, may or may not be developed, may or may not be stimulated by external influences. It thus concerns a vitally important quality that everyone must handle with utmost care. People have potential not only as employees of a business but also as personalities with a variety of private and public duties and spheres of influence.

Because potential is among those terms that have lost their clarity, having been trampled and hackneyed through extensive use, it is worth reflecting upon the actual meaning of the word. According to the 1963 *Duden Book of Etymology*, potential is 'innate capability, strength of the sphere of influence'. The word was first formed in the nineteenth century from the late Latin 'potentialis', meaning 'according to ability; having an active effect'.

Thus capacity, strength and ability can be truly immense or alternatively very small, or perhaps barely exist at all. Potential therefore does not necessarily describe 'great' or 'high' qualities; on the contrary it refers to something that is certainly always present, but that does not have predetermined intensities and effects. Moreover, its development does not always follow an upward or forward direction.

In *Man without Characteristics*, Robert Musil writes: 'There is no second such example of inescapability, than when a talented young person shrinks into a common old person.' Wasted, unused or nonexistent potential?

There are, on the other hand, many examples describing the exact opposite: people who unremittingly develop themselves personally, intellectually and professionally, who thus know how to raise their performance capacity and their capabilities. Potential is therefore clearly a quality that can be stimulated, increased, broadened and developed. It can also fall into ruin, wither away and contract.

For decades the author had the opportunity to observe the development of countless people, to accompany them, to work with them and to encourage them. Despite, or perhaps precisely because of, the great number of paths of development, rifts, incidents, high and low points, it is hard to pinpoint benchmarks that could be standardized and applied to others. People are unique to themselves and that also applies to their development.

> There is no simple 'technique' of personal development. There is, however, knowledge of contexts and principles, which can facilitate understanding and be of practical use.

The Three Pillars of the Development of Potential

Potential and the possibilities for its development depend on three fundamental pre-requisites:

- motivation and behaviour
- knowledge, abilities and experience
- organization and discipline.

It is desirable to look at these three 'cardinal elements' in more detail. This will be done from the viewpoint of personal development and of recognizing and developing the potential of employees for future tasks: in other words tasks different from those they do today.

Motivation and Behaviour

As we know, there is an exceedingly close relationship between motivation and behaviour. Motives and desires are the very qualities that trigger and govern behaviour. Motivation can have an external source (*extrinsic motivation*) and thus affect behaviour. In businesses these are by no means confined to consciously directed influences, such as training opportunities, career development possibilities, feedback through evaluation procedures, communication about strategies, successes, innovations, acquisitions, mission statements and many more. They also include influences that emerge by chance, agreeable to one individual, disagreeable to another, such as colleagues, subordinates and superiors. As positive or negative role models, opinion-formers, heroes or losers they can have a stimulating, inhibiting or otherwise influential effect.

Set against external factors are motives arising from personal tendencies. These include needs acquired during the course of development, and patterns of behaviour that meet those needs and that were adopted because they proved successful. Recalling McClelland, the need for success, power or a sense of belonging triggers different behaviour, affecting performance ability and capacity. This can be good, bad or indifferent, depending on the type of function, role or task it concerns.

People who have an intense need for clear and immediate proof of success offer little potential for contemplative, analytical, advisory or research-based tasks – even if they would be thoroughly 'suitable' in terms of formal training requirements. On the other hand, it can be presumed that the type of people who would enjoy such tasks would be looking to be part of an experienced team, in which professionally and intellectually they can constantly find new challenges. However, we might not without hesitation be able to say whether these people would have the potential to run a factory or win new customers.

> Motivation and behaviour are in some respects the 'software' of potential.

Knowledge and Abilities

> Knowledge, abilities and experience can be compared to the 'hardware'.

Software alone is unworkable and hardware alone is useless: both are necessary.

It is not enough to be 'motivated' in order to fulfil a task. *Knowledge* is also vital: knowledge, for example, of food chemistry, tax law, logistics, market research, information technology, machine construction, cost calculation. The list could be continued indefinitely, and not only because there are so many fields of knowledge, but also because they continually change and regenerate.

To apply knowledge successfully *abilities* are vital, for example in how to prioritize, plan, set targets, communicate, control, analyse, combine, evaluate, relativize and countless more besides.

One ability should be especially emphasized: the ability to learn! Without this ability, which includes the willingness to learn, knowledge and insights have only limited use.

Almost every insight and all knowledge that we have gained have truly short life spans. The 'half-life' of most knowledge, even if the fruit of extensive research, is mostly measured in years, not decades.

A study presented at the end of the 1990s by the Director General for Labour and Social Affairs of the European Union ascertained that 80 per cent of the knowledge used to perform today's jobs will become redundant between 2010 and 2015. Yet 80 per cent of the people who will then be in employment have already completed their formal schooling and academic training.

Even if these figures seem more impressive in terms of their symmetry than in their precision, they nevertheless illustrate plainly the value of the ability and willingness to learn – especially in terms of evaluating the potential to fulfil future tasks.

In the context of potential and its development *experience* is not insignificant, as it contributes primarily to personal maturity and to the development of faculties of judgement, social competence and cultural awareness. In terms of consolidating and broadening knowledge, however, experience must today make an increasingly declining contribution as knowledge very quickly becomes obsolete. Experience can also have a negative effect, because it often leads to well-worn ways of working and behaving that are not always up-to-the-minute or intelligent.

Organization and Discipline

It might perhaps come as a surprise or sound like an echo from long distant times of hierarchy and authority to mention organization and discipline in the context of discussing the development of potential. But this is not what is meant: here the idea is related to the *structure of our own lives*.

It is well known that some people tend to be 'unorganized', others are 'undisciplined', some are both, others in turn are neither. Whether or to what degree this represents inherent or acquired behaviour or needs is open to question. Whatever the source may be, it clearly influences our performance ability and capacity in fulfilling certain roles and performing certain tasks successfully.

Being unorganized or undisciplined is not always detrimental, and the opposite is not always advantageous. It is partly a question of degree, but mainly depends on where such qualities are brought into play.

Tasks demanding unconventional solutions, where new situations constantly arise, are generally less effectively managed by firmly structured, organized, disciplined, ordered and regimented thought and processes than by intuition, innovation and, if one will, a certain disorder: chaos as a principle of order!

> Motivation, behaviour, knowledge, abilities, organization, discipline are thus individual variables of potential, which in their different intensities create variously favourable or unfavourable conditions for successfully accomplishing certain tasks in certain areas of responsibility. There can therefore be no good or bad 'standard mixture'; it is, as the English would say, all about 'horses for courses'.

Additionally there is an associated influence arising from organization and discipline, namely the degree to which these qualities are embedded in the structure and processes of the business itself. An organizational structure is almost like a skeleton, affording stability and making sure all the various parts are held together. This then orders and channels information, communication, feedback, operations and processes. The organizational structure can – if set up efficiently – shed light on areas of responsibility and clarify the vertical and horizontal arrangement of a business and its departments. This internal transparency delineates for the employees possible paths of development from the lower to the higher levels of responsibility. Distinct organizational structure provides a clear picture of responsibility and accountability. Moreover, it endows the organization itself with greater significance, because it ultimately concerns the priorities that the organization puts upon its responsibilities to owners (e.g. the shareholders), employees, customers, suppliers, the state, society and interest groups (e.g. worker representatives, consumer groups, environmentalists).

Such considerations have certainly not always been important, nor did the same demands always exist. Originally, organizational structures expressed hierarchical structure: the 'lines of command' and the way in which work was distributed among the areas and levels of the business. The structures were therefore very rigid, arranged in pyramid form, and in essence the hierarchical structures of most businesses were very similar. In a 1993 publication, *Personnel Management in the New Europe*, the author wrote about organizational structure:

> In conclusion it can be stated that the 1970s and 1980s brought in the first instance a great variety of forms and later witnessed the departure of strict hierarchy, and that the early 1990s . . . took decisive steps away from structure and towards dynamism. . . . The principle of structure was perhaps not completely replaced by the principle of procedure, but it was certainly widely suppressed. Organizations were certainly less often conceived on a monolithic basis; rather, they more often grew in the direction of variety and adaptability. Structure as a mechanism or as a means for order and control, and above all as a principle of rank, has already lost its lustre and this will continue as businesses move towards being governed by procedure and spurred on by innovation. . . . Autonomy of individual departments, together with tighter strategic integration, is made more possible by a reduced emphasis on hierarchy and greater opportunities of communication due to more advanced communications technology.
>
> (Kressler, 1993, pp. 57, 65)

This indeed all took place exactly or very nearly as described. The dismantling of structures, however, has been and remains less embracing and definitive than many expected and predicted.

In a 1992 publication entitled *Competency Based Human Resource Management*, there is the proposition that in future organizations will become *clusters*. The authors argue:

> In this context employees are beginning to work in cluster organizations where people are not tied to a management level by traditional hierarchical lines. These clusters have a great amount of freedom in which to accomplish a mission given to them. The performance of these empowered clusters is measured on the accomplishment of the mission only.
>
> (Mitrani *et al.*, 1992, p. 18)

In reality this prognosis has been shown to be exaggerated. It runs the risk of obscuring responsibility for investing limited resources and accountability for setting feasible goals and developing products that can be competitive on the market. If a business is to be managed efficiently, internal control cannot be entirely relinquished. Some degree of organization and discipline is undoubtedly essential!

There are more rigid and more flexible organization structures, more stringent and more relaxed rules and standards of behaviour. These then shape the varying key issues of an organization's culture. Some organizations are more task-based, others more people-oriented; more formal or informal; more result-based or more procedure-based (more concerned about output, or more about input); more open or closed; keener to adhere to principles or more pragmatic; with a stronger emphasis on being a part of the business or with stronger emphasis on belonging to a specific discipline (G. Hofstede, *Cultures and Organizations, Software of the Mind*, examines organization culture in greater detail).

Returning to the question of performance capacity and the development of potential we can draw the conclusion that follows.

Different organizational parameters correspond to correspondingly different needs, preferences and motives. Some people find it easier to develop themselves and their performance capacity when the way they set about this is as far as possible up to them; others in turn need more protection and guidance. Where one prefers to pursue very specific results aggressively, the other is better placed tackling professionally more in-depth and intellectually perhaps more complex tasks. There are people who value a higher degree of formality because they are interested in status and perhaps are more reserved, whereas others would much rather be one among equals. Some strive for a dominating, leading role; others prefer to be subordinate, either to a system or to standards.

Potential and Ambition

The development of potential, and the potential for development: in either case, it has been seen that knowledge and abilities, organization and discipline are decisive criteria for motivation and behaviour.

In order to realize the potential for development and thus successfully develop potential it is important to be aware of how these variables are variously formed. They are grounded in individual differences that ensure that no two people can share precisely the same motivation and behaviour, knowledge and abilities, organization and discipline.

> Thus there are people with high potential and also those with low potential. There are people with greater or lesser ambition. Potential and ambition do not always run parallel. Those with great ambition and low potential must try to reconcile this discrepancy as best they can.

If it cannot be reconciled, then one of two situations will probably arise. There may be an excess of ambition, spurring the individual on to dreams that cannot be realized. The outcome will be failure, disappointment, frustration, and therefore on balance both life and career prove very dissatisfying. There might also be a more 'realistic' development, which adapts to the level of potential; in this case, however, the unremitting demands of unfulfilled ambition will cause all achievements to seem unsatisfactory, and thus this approach also leads to constant dissonance.

A discrepancy of the opposite type – that is, when potential is greater than ambition – creates a tension that, if not reconciled, also leads to dissonances, though of a different kind.

When the degree of potential agrees with the extent of ambition, then there is naturally nothing to reconcile and very little should stand in the way of harmonious development.

One can vividly portray ambition and potential in a system of coordinates, as shown in Figure 3.1. On the top right there is high potential

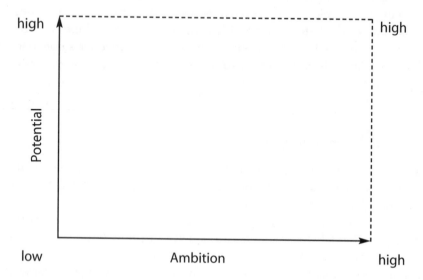

Figure 3.1. Ambition and potential

combined with high ambition and on the bottom left low potential and low ambition. In between every possible type of agreement or also discrepancy can be imagined.

It is vitally important that every person asks: 'What is the goal in my life, my job, what are my spiritual goals, what about my material ones. . .?' The next question proceeds: 'Can I accomplish these? What would I need to accomplish them? Can I get it? Where would I be best placed to get it?' The individual should not always try to answer these questions alone; people who are known and trusted can be of great assistance.

These questions, which are extremely difficult to answer, should aim first of all to create a certain balance between ambition and potential. If the attempt to fulfil potential is to prove successful, it is then also necessary to look for and find a way which makes achieving the goal seem most likely – for there are no guarantees.

> This process of agreement between ambition or aspiration and potential or promise should most sensibly be repeated and renewed at set intervals, as conditions and possibilities change over the course of time: both in the environment and in what seems obvious to the individual.

It was suggested earlier that choosing a course for one's life and career is dependent on the particular combination of drama, ritual and routine that one personally favours. A further variable is the relationship between potential and ambition.

Earlier, potential was discussed primarily as something peculiar to individual, as something highly personal – as indeed it is.

Businesses and other organizations, as well as the work and procedures of self-employment, provide diverse conditions for fulfilling and developing potential. The emphasis lies on *diverse*, not on good or bad. Whether it is good or bad is above all up to the individual, balancing potential and ambition on the one hand and the available conditions and requirements on the other.

This also partly explains why one's journey through life very seldom runs in line with one's career path and towards a goal that is established once and for all. Often – and with increasing frequency – goals and thus paths are adjusted. In a world of constant change, new possibilities and new undertakings are offered far more often than before, new opportunities are opened up, new lessons can or must be learnt and there are fresh opportunities and challenges. Changes can also often be unwelcome, requiring perhaps both an examination of new demands and a realignment of potential and ambition.

Everybody, whether working in a business, in public administration, in their own business, in an interest group, a political party, a church or wherever, will achieve something there, will contribute something – to the results, to accomplishing goals, to forming a culture, to teamwork. These achievements are set against demands that are relevant both today and in the future. Individuals contribute to the wider development and thereby always should, can or hope to promote their own personal development. It is not only considerations relating to material needs or status that prove decisive, but also the need for personal development, self-esteem and self-actualization (as Maslow suggested).

Potential as a Contribution

Relatively early on businesses, which in contrast to some other organizations have always been in intense competition for the right employee, were aware not only of the importance of motivation, abilities and performance, but also that these attributes could be further developed to meet ever-increasing demands. It very soon became evident that people differed not only in education, knowledge and experience, but also in creativity, innovation, organizational skills, communication, ability to handle stress, faculty of judgement, leadership, strategic thinking, and other qualities and characteristics. These proved difficult to define and even more difficult to measure. It was clear, however, that they were crucial factors that had a considerable influence on success and efficiency, particularly in highly qualified and responsible work, and ultimately on the ability to fulfil leading roles.

This was by no means a phenomenon unique to the industrial, hierarchical era. It applies even more strongly to the post-industrial and post-hierarchical world. Greater flexibility, more intense dynamism, the higher degree of internationalization, ubiquitous cultural diversity, the increasing influence of associated areas and the responsibility towards a large number of sophisticated and justifiably demanding stake holders – these and other factors make it ever more difficult to meet the conditions for making correct decisions and for successfully implementing every necessary procedure.

Selection is therefore intensified, with the criteria for appointment to more difficult and more responsible duties becoming both more vital and more demanding. That does not apply only to businesses, but to all organizations – or at least it should.

Criteria of Potential

Some people very clearly possess the characteristics or criteria that determine their potential to fulfil more difficult and more responsible tasks to a greater extent than others. In some businesses there has been a structured and systematic endeavour to find out how to identify and perhaps even measure these qualities. As already noted, the search for a ready-made and simple method of predicting future potential of performance levels from present functions or tasks proved to be unrewarding and often misleading.

Ascertaining criteria for potential, however, enabled a sounder basis to be established than by using intuition alone. It should be emphasized, however, that 'feeling' is not always deceptive, even when the 'strike rate' is perhaps not entirely convincing.

'Predictor Qualities'

In the 1960s an empirical study was conducted under the aegis of some large businesses in the Netherlands, to identify the characteristics, qualities and abilities that indicated a potential for development. This enabled so-called *predictor qualities* to be defined.

The method was as follows. First of all an inventory was drawn up, listing the widest possible range of qualities that could be found in employees who had proved to be successful. These findings and discoveries were then analysed and categorized. Finally, the results were checked in further investigations and through many discussions about their relevance. It must be remembered that the objective context was to find criteria that suggested the presence of the potential for development within the framework of business enterprises, and to identify qualities that enabled people in such businesses to rise from the lowest to the highest levels of responsibility and duties. It is certainly likely that, even if identical qualities are not decisive in fulfilling the potential for development in other types of organizations, then at least very similar ones are.

In practical terms, seven key criteria were identified for the purpose of evaluating potential within businesses.

1. *'Helicopter'-ability:* This describes the talent or art of being able to rise above the hubbub of everyday life from time to time, being able to look at the big picture, to perceive possible developments and strategic alternatives, and thus draw the right conclusions. Thus equipped, the 'helicopter' returns to earth, enabling suitable decisions

to be made and appropriate steps to be taken, which somebody who is not in the position to gain a broad overview is probably unable to do.

2. *Intellectual vitality:* It might perhaps seem surprising that four decades ago, when everything was 'so simple', this was already a serious matter. However, because we always feel that the world in which we live right now is the most complex of all possible worlds, animated and innovative thinking, unconventional resolution of problems (the emphasis is on *resolution*!), critical analysis, awareness and a thirst for knowledge have always been essential qualities for people who want and are able to be successful in responsible capacities with strategic importance and influence on long-term developments.

3. *Physical fitness:* The study demonstrated that not only intellectual animation is important, but also the physical ability to withstand stress. As a rule, less directly physical effort is required as duties acquire increased responsibility. Yet increased responsibility is certainly associated with more severe stress factors, which, as is well known, can cause all kinds of tangible strain and physical symptoms. This then bears on the whole ability to perform, including both physical and intellectual aspects, which indeed cannot really be separated from each other. Having to endure endless meetings is a physical effort that should not be underestimated. Constant travel causes even greater stress, especially when it involves travelling over different time zones. To save time people mostly travel by plane. As airports are becoming increasingly busy, delays increasingly frequent and the planes ever more uncomfortable, travelling itself is already an unrelenting fitness exercise.

Juvenal's most misquoted and misunderstood phrase *Orandum est ut sit mens sana in corpore sano* (Your prayer must be that you may have a sound mind in a sound body) is very appropriate here.

4. *Charisma:* Carrying out responsible functions generally requires the ability to lead, convince and 'motivate' others. It thus stretches beyond the immediate subordinates, who acknowledge a formal order of authority in the hierarchical relationship. Apart from the fact that merely giving orders in no way constitutes an effective form of leadership, it is completely counterproductive for all those who, using their own initiative as far as possible, can and should help to accomplish a task, conclude a project or resolve a problem.

The ability to formulate goals and to inspire others to adopt them as their own, making them the object of their own ambition, is an important prerequisite to galvanize and pull together resources for optimal effect. These resources may take the form of intellectual capacity or professional capability, and often lie latent in the talents of the people in the business. Charisma is about stimulating people by tapping into their enthusiasm, which is altogether different from exercising formal authority, coercion, threats or even using 'incentives' of a financial sort or otherwise. The term 'charisma' derives from the Greek and originally meant 'graciousness', or denoted the intellectual strength that especially empowers its bearer to lead the community. From a sociological point of view it describes the extraordinary abilities of a talented leader to establish a relationship of authority in such a way that the subordinates follow with personal commitment and enthusiasm. This means that the almost magical effect of charisma does not long outlive the success of the leader or the followers. Napoleon was such a charismatic leader but, even for him, only until his star began to wane.

In the more everyday practice of managing businesses and other organizations, charisma is now also spoken of in connection with less extraordinary talents of leadership and enthusiasm.

5. *Tenacity:* As a task increases in responsibility, it usually also involves more complex matters. Moreover, the changes, innovations, new strategic directions and structural adjustments that must be introduced and implemented are greater and more far-reaching than in jobs that are less significantly influential. Innovation and change are very often met with scepticism, suspicion and even rejection. The unknown is plagued with greater risks than the familiar. Therefore, as a consequence of all the uncertainty, there are also many arguments against change. Even well thought-out and well grounded alterations do not always receive unanimous approval; indeed they much more often meet with vehement rejection, at least on the part of those who feel unsettled or even threatened by them. Hence people do not always lay their cards on the table: 'spin' and *ruses de guerre* are employed in order to influence, to limit, and to prevent. As well as skill and sound argument, therefore, enforcing necessary changes also often demands considerable tenacity.

The author was often reminded – as surely were many other people who enforced changes – of Machiavelli's (1446–1507) advice to princes: 'Nothing is more difficult, dangerous or of uncertain success than assuming the leadership at the beginning of a new order; for the innovator is the enemy of everyone who flourished under the previous conditions, and has only half-hearted support from all those who might benefit from the change.'

That is but one aspect illustrating why tenacity is a significant criterion in evaluating potential. Another is that tasks with greater responsibility are mostly long term. The higher the function, the more strategic will be its composition. This means that it will contain more medium and long-term duties and will entail fewer manual and short-term activities. Because the nature of medium and long-term goals means that their suitability can only be assessed after some time, it is vital to maintain the desired course and insist on the necessary measures by demonstrating other qualities including (and especially) tenacity.

6. *Need for power:* In discussing McClelland's theory of motivation mention was made of the need for power as one of the three most cogent needs that trigger certain behaviour in order to satisfy them.

   Similarly, the need for power has been recognized as one of the most important criteria for potential. This has nothing to do with being greedy for power, but concerns a pronounced, but at the same time balanced, yearning to be able to influence, to assert oneself, to determine developments, to form opinions, to be noticed, to gain status, to take charge of situations and to dominate. The behaviour that will realize these conceptions and goals also to a large degree fulfils the demands exacted by responsible functions. The need for power then predicates upon the functionality of behaviour, not upon a superficial aspiration for the power, status and prestige that come with higher positions.

   Determining whether someone has the potential to perform leading roles does not depend on whether they hanker after power, which is only a superficial part of the matter. Rather it depends on whether they fundamentally, and not only in a narrow professional sense, want to fulfil the desire explained in the previous paragraph as the 'need for power', and then cultivate the necessary behaviour, qualities and talents to do so. Need and desire alone are not nearly enough. The determination and ability to be able to satisfy the need are also required.

   When this form of the need for power is absent, however, then there is an insufficient motivating force, no initial spark to trigger the behaviour that helps to spur someone on to rise to more responsible positions.

7. *Humanity:* Responsibility, power and leadership are attributes that gain in significance and weight during the course of career development and professional progress. They are above all associated with intransigence, aggression, coldness, even ruthlessness. It is evident, however, that for sustained successful advancement a dose of sympathy for human weaknesses, some warmth, compassion and empathy are also important to secure continued success.

It is especially prudent in managerial positions to pay the human dimension just as much attention as points concerning technical aspects and the management and policies of the business. At management level, strategic and organizational decisions and changes are instigated that affect people and their interests, hopes, expectations, vulnerabilities and fears. This does not call for soft-heartedness, irresolution or a lack of economic realism, but for a sense of balance, the ability to see the bigger picture, a consideration of all major influences, both the damaging and the beneficial ones, which ultimately all combine to determine success or failure.

In this context the term 'humanity' can easily be misunderstood. It has nothing to do with avoiding all unpleasantness, wanting to do the right thing by everybody, only bearing good tidings, always searching for a consensus. That would not only be unrealistic, irresponsible and weak, but also in the long term not quite so humane as was perhaps intended or might have appeared. Unfortunately changes are not only unavoidable but must even be actively pursued and stimulated, in order to secure not only the survival of the firm, the business or the organization, but also the ability to compete, grow and succeed. To hold such changes in check because the consequences may entail human discomfort is economically irresponsible and harmful to the people concerned, and furthermore short-sighted and opportunistic. Human dilemmas that have been avoided will have to be addressed at some later stage, with more inescapable consequences and at an even higher cost, because reality has the astonishing knack of reining in even the most idealistic of dreams.

None the less, the humanitarian approach does have a great impact, not so much on what is done as on how it is done. When economic circumstances make it inevitable that a factory will close, it can hardly be sensible to ignore this for 'humanitarian' reasons; that would be – as described above – short-sighted, unrealistic, opportunistic and ultimately also not very 'humane'. The inevitable closure can, however, either be carried out in such a way that people feel the full force of the harsh consequences, or with an attempt to soften the blow as far as possible. In the first instance, all the necessary measures will be taken to dismiss all of the workers in one fell swoop, pay compensation and send everyone their 'cards' on the day before closure. This might satisfy the financial obligations, but the people affected would be catastrophically let down in an inhumane way. (This is a simplified account because, in practice, laws giving rights to extensive information, hearings and co-determination must often be adhered to.) The same financial means can, however, be used to provide opportunities for retraining, to set up measures for outplacement or to offer career advice and general guidance for living. Instead of a ruthlessly hard crash, a soft landing has thus been made possible and the human needs that have arisen from the economic necessity have as far as possible been met.

Putting these criteria to practical use has over the course of time proved well worthwhile, even if assessing the potential for development has only been possible qualitatively and not quantitively, and even then more as an art than a technique. Knowledge of the relevant criteria and characteristics, however, provides a very handy intellectual tool.

It should be remembered that *relevance* is a relative term; the author was able to verify this again, as it has been proposed that these criteria, which were first drawn up in the Netherlands, should also be put to use in England. Indeed, some headway could be made with them in England, although one trait was missed that certainly plays a far more significant role in English culture than on the European continent, namely a 'sense of humour'.

Competencies

In the 1990s there was an interesting development, namely a method of assessing competence that opened up a new approach to appraising performance ability, to 'predicting' performance capacity and thus also to evaluating potential.

Before this method is examined more closely, it is advisable first to consider the terminology. Applying 'competencies' as criteria for evaluating the potential of both performance and development involves not a simple 'technique' but the intelligent use of well-understood terms. The *Duden Etymology* describes 'competent' as 'responsible, definitive, authoritative'. The word originates from the legal language of the eighteenth century and has Latin roots (*competere:* to be correct, fitting, appropriate). *Competence* is the corresponding noun and in official language denotes a sense of responsibility.

Because the development of the *Competency Assessment Method*, in which David McClelland played a leading role (see the section on motivation, pages 23–5) took place in America, the Anglo-American use of the term is worth noting. In UK English, *competence* means ability, capability, suitability, proficiency, qualification, appropriateness, while *competency* means '(sufficient) income to live on' (*Collins English Dictionary*). According to

Webster's New Encyclopaedic Dictionary, *competence* means 'sufficient for the necessities of life' and 'the quality or state of being competent'. Referring then to *competent* we find 'having the necessary ability or qualities'; 'legally qualified'. In *Webster's* there is no difference between *competence* and *competency*.

Competence or competency: a common conceptual denominator embracing at least ability, qualification, legitimacy/proficiency on the basis of acquired and verified knowledge, qualities and talents, capability to fulfil a task, or being responsible (competent) on account of relevant understanding and personal aptitude. Because a list of all of these distinguishing characteristics can be unwieldy and confusing, it is easier to conform to a convention of language usage: in *Faust* Goethe writes: 'When phrases founder, one word can come to the rescue.' This helpful word is *competency*.

In the context of this book competency will not be used in the sense suggested by the *Collins English Dictionary*. The booklet *Competency Assessment Methods* by David McClelland, Lyle M. Spencer and Signe M. Spencer, provides the following definition: "A competency is defined as an underlying characteristic of an individual which is causally related to effective or superior performance in a job."

These competencies were then put into groups to facilitate catgorization in a recognizable system. The competencies identified were:

- Motives: it will perhaps come as no surprise that the need for achievement is one such motive (see McClelland's theory of motivation, pages 23–5).
- Characteristics: for example self-confidence and self-discipline.
- Personal moral concepts.
- Knowledge of facts, processes and procedures.
- Specific abilities: for example, seeing connections or drawing conclusions.

By critically evaluating the identified competencies it was possible to ascertain which ones contributed decisively to exceptional performance capacity ('differentiating competencies') and also the minimum composition necessary to guarantee an acceptable or average level of performance.

The method of ascertaining differentiating competencies can be applied specifically to businesses if it is assumed that, to ensure success and high performance, different businesses and organizations also call for specifically different competencies alongside the usual ones. Depending on the line of business and nature of the work, a whole array of differentiating competencies can be discovered.

There are various ways to determine the relevant competencies. Experience has shown the author that it is worthwhile to glance into the future: the question remains which strategic directions, which priorities and which challenges are to be expected in the future. One can derive the prospective differentiating competencies from the answer. At the same time it is possible to identify the currently verifiable differentiating competencies. This can be done by listing all of the competencies and comparing clearly above-average and successful employees with those who are rather more middling. Success in this instance denotes persistently achieving goals, as well as further contributions to the development of the business, the ability to learn and undertake self-improvement and, in due course, the ability to accomplish increasingly responsible tasks with sustained above-average success.

It does not seem apt to cite further examples of particular specific competencies, as it is always only in a given context that they can be identified as more or less differentiating. Discussing them in an abstract sense may be misleading rather than revealing. General examples have already been cited above.

Heroes, Prophets and Magicians

As already stated in the introduction, current performance does not reliably indicate future performance ability; just as little can be read from success at school or in further education. It is again emphasized that neither aspect is irrelevant, but by themselves they cannot paint the complete picture. That has been known for decades and has resulted in numerous studies, some more intuitive than others, some more empirical, of hidden and reliable indicators. One such study came up with the previously mentioned assortment of abilities and qualities from which future performance potential can be derived.

Somewhat less systematic was – and still is – the orientation in many businesses around leading figures. Every business, every organization has its 'heroes', 'prophets' and 'magicians'. They can often to be assigned to the category of 'charismatic leaders' (this incidentally reflects the meaning of the word, for in fact charisma originally signified a supernatural gift to accomplish inexplicable and wonderful feats).

In the main these heroes, prophets and magicians demonstrate highly developed qualities that distinguish their extraordinary feats, their impact and their triumphs. The characteristics and types of behaviour that emerge as particularly forceful criteria for success are generally few in number and are not that uncommon, but are consequently all the more marked. Such characteristics might include an especially convincing ability to communicate, an unusual gift for reading trends in the market, uniquely critical thought coupled with high creativity, an outstanding ability to encourage and inspire others, unrivalled specialized knowledge, extraordinary dynamism, an infallible feeling for success, the 'Midas touch' whereby everything is turned to gold (without the disadvantage which proved the undoing of the mythical King Midas) and a whole lot more besides.

The behavioural patterns and character profiles of the heroes, prophets and magicians are very often consciously (though also frequently subconsciously) cited as a model and yardstick for measuring the future potential of employees as they rise to the top.

Hence there is yet another factor playing a not insignificant role, namely the tendency of those with authority, responsibility or influence in a business or organization to look for new people or even successors who correspond to their own personal profile. There is thus a frequent tendency to replicate characteristics, behaviour and qualities that have already been acknowledged as successful. This is very easy to explain and justify, as behavioural patterns that have already been proved in this specific business, in this particular market and in this situation are bound to provide easily accessible and concrete reference points. This must necessarily be more relevant than concepts that are generally viable, but are therefore more abstract.

The practice illustrated above is often rewarding and thus should never be rejected outright. It becomes questionable only when it continues to be uncritically and thoughtlessly maintained even when the environmental conditions, the markets and the demands change. Replication then becomes dangerous, missing the opportunity to look for new competencies that better correspond to the changed conditions than the ones that have been hitherto so successful.

Sometimes the tendency to maintain the status quo is so powerful that it takes a crisis to replace old patterns with new ones. The signs of and causes for change are often restructuring, a merger, a change in ownership or a different management team.

Potential: For What?

In the era of hierarchies most businesses and other types of organizations were largely structured in the form of a pyramid. A hierarchical diagram portrayed the levels and the 'floors' of the pyramid. At the same time it depicted the distribution of authority, responsibility and status, outlined where the highest, the high, the middle and the lower management positions were placed, and which level was inhabited by the people who carried out the practical tasks, namely the base of the pyramid. Often the job title alone would indicate a particular level. The career ladder was thus also just as clearly delineated.

These very rigid structures were a throwback to the traditions of the church and military. Over the course of time, however, they became more and more flexible, the job content followed less and less the logic of hierarchy, the structures, once dominated by command and control, were transformed and became more and more relaxed. Self-responsibility, autonomy and *empowerment* shifted the main emphasis away from the formal order of rank and increasingly towards the individual, who now created jobs rather than having to adapt to them. The number of hierarchical levels was radically reduced, initiating a new distribution of the responsibility.

Now that the career ladder is harder to discern, status should not play such a dominant role from either the business's or the individual's point of view. Nevertheless two requirements are as true as they ever were. First, in businesses there are tasks that make very different demands. Second, in their lives, their careers and in their work most people want to see positive results, progress, growth and advancement.

It is vital that both points of view objectively determine the distinct values of various tasks in the business. This enables the business to offer people tasks according to their actual abilities and their potential; at the same time the staff have the opportunity to set the standard for their own professional development. If a business is successful in continually offering people tasks that correspond to their capacities, then both objectives will be met: that of the efficiency of the business, and that of the personal and professional development of the employee.

There is a whole host of methods to measure levels of responsibility, demands and the significance of tasks. However, this opens up an entirely different theme, which we will not consider at this point.

Performance and Potential

To round off this chapter it is desirable to cast a brief glance at the relationship between performance and potential.

As an illustration a simple graph has proved worthwhile (Figure 3.2). Much like the possible combinations of potential and ambition in Figure

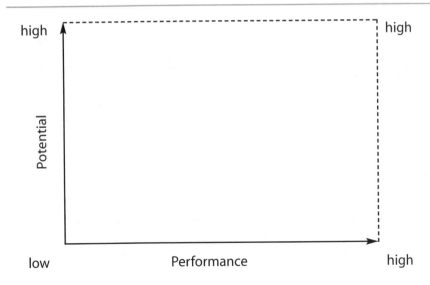

Figure 3.2. Potential and performance

3.1, here too there are all manner of conceivable variations ranging from high to low potential and high to low performance. An individual placed in the top right corner – one who combined high performance with high potential – would, using the terminology of portfolio analysis, be a 'star'. There are, however, other combinations.

Another extreme case – bottom left – is also feasible. This might represent somebody who at the moment is in the wrong job, but in another capacity would perhaps have more to offer (there are, however, many other possible reasons for being positioned here).

A simple overview like the one depicted above can at least enable an initial file to be drafted. This draft should certainly not be considered authoritative, but should be substantially expanded as time goes on. By putting forward ideas and demonstrating ways to evaluate potential, this section can thus offer helpful support. Again it is emphasized that applying analytical 'techniques' to evaluate potential is no guarantee of success. Imagination and intuition also play a part and, above all, so does understanding the source of the capacity for future performance.

CHAPTER 4

Evaluation in Practice

A Real-life Example

A real-life example may serve to illustrate how the building blocks of an evaluation system that embraces both performance and potential might be put together. The example, selected from a business we will call 'Optima', contains all the significant elements without being overwhelmingly comprehensive. It is often counterproductive to overload a system with too many elements. Such a system may well promise more information, and greater depth and precision of results, but it can easily become so unwieldy for its users (the evaluator and the evaluation subject), so difficult to comprehend and time-consuming, that it is never fully accepted.

The following elements from Optima's evaluation system will be examined:

- evaluation principles
- annual performance appraisal
- some explanations to improve understanding of both areas
- the evaluation process.

Optima's Evaluation Principles

1. OBJECTIVES

Success, growth and sustained competitive ability are achieved in Optima to a very high degree through the capacity and willingness to perform of all its employees and through their competency. It is therefore useful and necessary to evaluate the performance and potential of all employees regularly and according to sensible principles and relevant criteria.

In terms of the measures undertaken by both the business and the employees, this evaluation should lead to more purposeful training, development and career planning.

Strengths should thus be maximized and weaknesses minimized, resulting in an optimal level of performance.

2. THE PARTIES CONCERNED

The management requires information about performance and development potential so as to determine how the present and also future endeavours of all of the employees compare to their ability and competency, and furthermore to provide appropriate training possibilities. To do this it is necessary to be aware of the employees' wishes, ambitions or even reservations.

The individual employees have a right to know the effort expected of them to achieve the business objectives; the skills that are especially relevant and should be developed; and the opportunities for personal and professional development in the company.

A well functioning evaluation system will be seen as an important building block for the success of the business and the personal success of all employees. All parties concerned – the management and employees on all levels and in all areas – will therefore undoubtedly do all they can to ensure that Optima's evaluation system is applied as effectively as possible.

3. RESPONSIBILITY FOR EVALUATION

Both the evaluator and the subject of the evaluation are responsible for applying the system. Although it is generally up to the superior to initiate the evaluation, the subordinate may also prompt it. In any case all of the employees in Optima have a right to be evaluated according to the rules of the system.

To ensure that uniform standards of evaluation have been maintained and that the process has been as objective as possible the evaluation results are corroborated at the immediately higher level.

The personnel managers who are responsible for particular areas of the business will, if necessary, lend support in applying the evaluation system.

Should an evaluation cause a disagreement that cannot be satisfactorily resolved even at the next level up from the evaluator, then the member of the management in Optima responsible for personnel policy will begin a process of arbitration.

4. THE PROCESS OF PERFORMANCE EVALUATION

The period between evaluations is usually one business year, which is the same as one calendar year.

The aims that are set and agreed upon in advance for the period of evaluations form the basis for the performance evaluation.

It is advisable to have occasional progress controls and progress reports throughout the year, so that steps can be taken to ensure that the aims remain achievable, even if unexpected obstacles should arise.

Once they have been agreed upon, aims can only be altered in exceptional circumstances, for example when a fundamental adjustment in the business strategy requires it or when unpredictable external changes make the originally determined goal no longer seem sensible.

The evaluator and the subject of the evaluation will in any case discuss the annual performance evaluation. The result will be put in writing by the evaluator, including a summary of the evaluation review. The evaluation subject can make written comments as well as add wishes and recommendations.

Particular attention should be given to the measures that have been planned or recommended on the strength of the evaluation.

The evaluation should take place as early as possible during the first week of the year.

5. PERFORMANCE AND POTENTIAL

The effort, contribution and results produced in the year's work form the essence of performance evaluations. Particular attention is paid to the extent to which the agreed objectives have actually been reached, under-achieved or surpassed. The evaluation should, however, also encompass any achievements that are not in the remit of the objectives.

Shortcomings also form part of the evaluation, especially how to rectify them.

The level of performance can occasionally intimate the potential of an employee for promotion to some higher position. What that particular position should be, however, is not always evident. Performance is immediate and concrete, and can be measured with reasonable reliability. Potential however can at best be estimated, but not measured, and should not be viewed as a prediction or a promise. It must therefore be assessed as something fundamentally distinct from performance.

In performance evaluations the evaluator will be asked for an opinion about the further development potential of the evaluation subject. This information should, however, at most be understood as an indication. The immediately higher level or even the level above that will pay close attention to placing the information in the framework of career and development strategies.

6. PERFORMANCE AND PAY

The Optima payment policy differentiates rewards according to responsibility, performance and success. The basic wage for every job is graded within a framework according to the level of responsibility. The result of the performance evaluation influences this grade. Part of the reward system is based on success, and this takes the form of bonus payments for achieving specific quantitative business objectives.

The annual evaluation review should not, however, involve financial arrangements and in any case should already have been conducted before these arrangements are made.

7. POTENTIAL AND PAY
Potential for a higher position generally has no direct influence on the current level of pay. As soon as someone is promoted to a higher position, however, the relevant payment methods should be brought into play.

8. FREQUENCY OF EVALUATION
Disregarding interim reviews and feedback, performance evaluations will as a rule be conducted annually. Should an employee have been working only for a short time, it may be appropriate to defer an evaluation until the next scheduled occasion.

Evaluating potential, when it is not covered by performance evaluation, is conducted at irregular intervals, primarily when decisions about important steps in career strategies have to be made or when a choice has to be made between two candidates for a key position.

Optima: Annual Performance Appraisal

1. FUNCTION
Name and other details
2. OVERALL EVALUATION
On the basis of the responsibility, area of the work, objectives and priorities, summarize performance, achievements during the course of the year and, if necessary, things not achieved:

3. EVALUATION CRITERIA

Solving problems
Analytical thought; ability to draw practical conclusions and simplify complex matters; imaginativeness; creativity and innovation; ability and willingness to learn (both formal learning and learning from experience and situations):

Assessment: exceptional / very good / meets relevant criteria / in need of improvement

Efficiency
Planning and implementing measures; utilizing resources; optimizing costs and yield; keeping to deadlines; quality and quantity:

Assessment: exceptional / very good / meets relevant criteria / in need of improvement

Motivation
Willingness to perform; effort; dynamism; initiative; stamina; ability to withstand stress:

Assessment: exceptional / very good / meets relevant criteria / in need of improvement

Leadership
Ability to convince; credibility; staying power; communication; control; feedback; faculty of judgement; ability to encourage; charisma:

Assessment: exceptional / very good / meets relevant criteria / in need of improvement

Team Skills
Understanding and listening to others; openness to ideas; cooperation and working alongside others; putting the job first; promotion of team spirit:

Assessment: exceptional / very good / meets relevant criteria / in need of improvement

Knowledge and Abilities
Professional competence; understanding the area of the business; technological knowledge; knowledge of customers and the market; keeping pace with latest developments; understanding and implementing strategies; entrepreneurial spirit:

Assessment: exceptional / very good / meets relevant criteria / in need of improvement

4. THE EVALUATOR'S RECOMMENDATIONS

Training:

Further career developments:

Miscellaneous:

5. RECOMMENDATIONS BY THE SUBJECT OF THE EVALUATION

Job content:

Responsibility:

Training:

Further career developments:

Miscellaneous:

6. OVERALL EVALUATION OF PERFORMANCE

Very good

Good

In need of improvement

No evaluation made (reasons):

7. POTENTIAL

Could assume a higher position within the next three years (please specify a few examples):

Could assume another position of the same level within the next three years (please specify a few examples):

Should stay in this position for at least the next three years:

Is not presently in the appropriate position:

8. EVALUATOR'S SUMMARY OF THE EVALUATION REVIEW

Date: Signature:

9. SUMMARY OF THE EVALUATION REVIEW BY THE SUBJECT OF THE EVALUATION

Date: Signature:

The evaluator's superior:

Additional comments:

Date: Signature:

Explanation of Optima's Evaluation Principles

These principles were devised by an internal team with the support of an external expert as the evaluation system was being introduced. Before the heads of management formally committed themselves to the principles as an evaluation strategy, they were discussed at all levels and in all areas of the business, and correspondingly adapted and changed. Thus from the outset not only was transparency ensured, but also identification and engagement with the process.

Every employee possesses a copy of the principles, and new entrants receive it in their 'starter pack'.

Performance and evaluation are based on objectives that are individually determined from the outset. In deciding on them, however, it is important to understand that these objectives must be suited to the content of the job and also accord with the aims of the business, although they are not identical with objectives used in the bonus system. The latter are based on results and are quantitatively determined; they also very often do not discriminate between members of a particular management level or business area when they are based on, for example, profit, turnover, growth or costs.

Objectives are more strongly personalized for performance evaluations. They also offer wider scope for qualitatively defined goals. They embrace both 'what' the crucial results of a given performance are, and especially 'how' the performance has been achieved, covering matters such as management behaviour, efficiency, the way customers or authorities have been treated, communication, knowledge enrichment and the development of employees' skills.

Performance is seen as distinct from potential; nevertheless it is expected that the evaluator will encourage development and comment on potential. The latter is important because the immediate superiors are best placed to report on their subordinates. However, the superior's proposals should not be accepted uncritically, as higher levels are by nature better placed to provide an overview of the composition, demands and conditions of different jobs. Care should be taken not to take the evaluator's report on the possible development potential of the subject as binding. Neither should a report that is perhaps too conservative or negative lead to the hasty conclusion that there are few prospects for the evaluation subject.

A crucial issue is how performance evaluation ties in with pay. Optima consciously circumscribes the pay scale for individual jobs, thus limiting the possibility of using significant variations in pay grades to reflect differences in performance. It has been proved, however, that this is not detrimental to the pursuit of a good evaluation, because good evaluations are above all viewed as an important contribution to further development or to consolidating one's position. Hence it is beneficial for result-based bonus payments (assuming that the results are in fact achieved) to form a significant component of performance within the overall payment scheme.

The 'harmonization' of the evaluation criteria among various business areas and levels demands a great deal of patience and can achieve only partial success. It would certainly be foolish to disregard evaluations that have been produced through a conscientious application of the principles and the system on the basis that they do not lend themselves well to a strict classification. The task remains a balancing act between sensible harmonization and necessary standardization.

The two major practical problems in applying the evaluation system are, first, the lack of time either to devise the annual evaluation or to conduct the reviews, and second, how to formulate objectives that correspond to the needs of the job and the individual, and that can also be measured qualitatively.

Explanation of the Annual Performance Evaluation in Optima

Evaluation criteria are chosen according to what is seen as relevant for the business. Not every element of the evaluation, however, is valid for every job, so it is not necessary to comment in detail on each one. On the other hand, it is equally likely that requirements other than the ones stipulated – which are given for guidance only – will become relevant.

After the evaluation review it is necessary that each criterion of the evaluation is briefly assessed, using the phrases *exceptional, very good, meets relevant criteria* or *in need of improvement*. Most of the assessments fall into the upper two categories. Care is taken, however, to avoid insisting upon a standard statistical spread (so-called 'forced distribution'). This precludes irritating control by a third party and ultimately also ensures that the evaluator must be able to justify the assessment. Somewhat imbalanced results do not therefore pose any major questions.

Main Points of the Evaluation Process in Optima

1. Towards the end of the previous year or at the beginning of the new year:
    – objectives are agreed upon for the coming year.
2. During the year:
    – there are occasional progress controls and regulatory measures;
    – only in exceptional cases should objectives be altered.

3. Towards the end of the year or beginning of the new year:
   – devise the annual evaluation;
   – produce the evaluation review;
   – evaluator and subject of evaluation both report;
   – agree upon new objectives for coming year.
4. 'Harmonization' of evaluation criteria and possible changes.
5. Recommendations and results of the evaluation are further utilized for training, career strategies and determining pay

PART III

Reward Strategies and Incentive Systems

CHAPTER 5

Structural Conditions for Reward

Overview

The terms 'reward', 'remuneration' and 'pay' are in essence very closely linked to what employees contribute, and what they get in return. They invoke different ideas for different people, however. For some they stand primarily for costs; others associate reward with motivation and recognition or, depending on an individual's personal experience, with frustration and disappointment; others in turn see pay in the first instance in the context of decency and fairness; for some pay is vital for leisure time and recreation; many see the level of their pay as an expression of their success. In some cultures, for example in North America, the notion of 'net worth' is often used. This is measured by totalling individual property and personal income by using the popular parallel of the way in which the market or share value of a business is assessed; 'net worth' is seen to stand roughly shoulder to shoulder with moral worth and intellectual capacity in the human scale of values. There is no desire here to fall into a moralizing tone, but to accept that a term that might appear unambiguous can have a substantial number of meanings.

> Whatever the individual and cultural variations, reward, along with the strategies and systems related to it, forms a significant part of a business's personnel policy. It can appeal to both the material and immaterial values of employees. Entrepreneurs and managers perceive in reward strategies a unique challenge and opportunity to make the most of what employees can contribute and be offered in return, in order to increase the potential of the net product.

In the language of business English and even in everyday language, the most widely used term is *reward*. It is clearly more descriptive than *pay* and indicates 'earnings; acquired, appropriate payment'. Hence *reward* has more positive overtones than the once much more common *remuneration*, which is reminiscent of the Latin word *munerare* (to give) or *munus* (a present). In American English *compensation* was and still is the popular term; this, however, invokes connotations of compensation for an endured hardship.

Professionalism and Emotion in Rewards

Experts in personnel, HR and remuneration place reward policy in a direct conceptual relationship with general business strategies and the consequent priorities of personnel policy. They devise reward strategies, therefore, that are mainly geared to setting and differentiating pay according to performance, potential, responsibility and results. The author is familiar with many such reward policy systems in numerous businesses. All, or nearly all, are characterized by logic, rationality and consistency. Enormous progress has been made during the last 20 or 30 years in this area, which is just as important as it is difficult. There are now very few leading businesses that do not have a 'state of the art' reward policy.

How is it, then, that this subject continues to offer a wide arena for debate, controversy, and indeed even for experimentation? The simple answer is that despite all the steps taken by all of the parties involved towards the goal of objectivity, fairness and all round agreement upon the costs and effects of reward, the final solution always seems to be one further step away.

It may be that these values, which seem absolute, are in constant opposition to the subjective nature of human perception, which relativizes everything and thus is the only single 'absolute'.

In *Gulliver's Travels* Jonathan Swift, a keen observer of human weaknesses and vanities, had in the eighteenth century already portrayed the efforts of the scholars at the scientific academy of Laputa to make their leaders 'choose favourites upon the score of their wisdom, capacity and virtue; of rewarding merit, great abilities and eminent services; of choosing for employment persons qualified.' Gulliver dismisses such notions as impossible, extravagant and irrational ideals.

A good 200 years later things are not quite so bad, but we do not seem to have yet found all the answers. It was not a satirical novelist but a leading management expert who, not all that long ago, chose as the subtitle to a chapter on 'Influencing Through Pay and Performance Appraisal' the simple words 'Toil and Trouble'. This was Harold J. Leavitt in the book *Readings in Managerial Psychology*. Leavitt states the following about these tools of management:

These are messy, difficult, double-edged tools that as often as not yield unintended negative changes along with the intended positive ones. They often generate frustration, anger, sabotage, gamesmanship and cut-throat competition. But somehow organizations can't seem to get along without them.

(Leavitt, 1980)

Despite all of the controversy and apparently irresolvable conflicts and antagonisms, businesses have no other choice than to continue searching for new, better and more intelligent approaches, which as far as possible correspond to both the business objectives and the ambitions, expectations and moral concepts of the employees and everybody else concerned.

Components of Reward

Reward as remuneration for the effort and results of work encompasses a variety of elements. The term 'reward' first and foremost brings financial matters to mind, that is, 'pay'. It must be emphasized, however, that pay is not the only form of reward. Indeed it is occasionally argued that financial payment is not even the most effective form of reward.

> It is beyond doubt that non-financial measures can form a very significant part of overall reward strategies in a more developed sense. Their nature does make them perhaps difficult to calculate and measure, but without doubt they have a high potential to stimulate performance, identification and abilities. Career development, promotion, feedback, communication and recognition can provide clear and effective indications of how performance is rewarded.

The wide-ranging definition of motivation and performance in this book therefore stretches from potential through to reward, as components of an interrelating whole. In the following pages reward will be discussed in a more specific sense: payments expressed in money or in monetary values.

In Europe and in all other industrial regions of the world, money is the component that is most directly related to reward. It can be fixed or variable, be immediately payable or deferred. The basic pay is a typical 'fixed component'. However, it is in the main not absolutely and permanently fixed; it tends to change at certain intervals, perhaps annually, according to performance and market trends. The 'variable component' usually encompasses short or long-term business results or the achievement of objectives that have been specifically set for a particular job or individual. Payment can ensue immediately – that is as soon as the period of the performance evaluation expires – or it can be deferred and made to depend upon other supplementary performance criteria or upon continued employment in the business for a given period.

This overview deliberately aims to avoid an over-simplistic fixation on the term 'incentive'. There have always been, however, more or less intelligent and interesting debates on the sense or folly of ideas about the stimulating or even motivating character of incentives. Among other things these debates discuss the lack of conclusive evidence about the relationship between stick, carrot and success and also the behavioural problems and misunderstandings which often arise.

These questions have been thoroughly discussed in the section on motivation and incentives. Here it is only important to note that the nature of incentives or stimuli is not so much a matter of the appropriate means, but rather more depends upon the disposition of the individual as a 'receiver'. Evidently, 'incentives' appeal positively to some people and engender a corresponding reaction. Others in turn find the ideas implied in incentives, namely that certain behaviour can be bought or that someone's behaviour might be unsuitable, acutely insulting. As has been argued elsewhere, it is an error to treat incentives and motivation as equivalents. Incentives function with regularity,

Stick and carrot

emitting the impetus and spur for targeted and highly specific actions, aims or activities; a certain performance or action looks towards the promise of an agreed reward for it. 'When you do that / achieve that / reach this goal, then you will get this' (wage increase, premium, bonus, additional holiday, airline tickets, or whatever). The employees' contribution and what they are offered in return are precisely calculated and, once the work is completed, the dues are settled. It is not necessary to provide a long list of evidence for the effectiveness of incentives – but only as impetus, not as motivation.

Motivation is constant, a sum of the desires and needs that crucially underpin people's behaviour and attitude towards work, achieving tasks and mapping out life's journey. Therefore motivation differs from incentives, for it can influence basic behaviour and offer personal perspectives some specific values.

A very important point to grasp from the following section is that overall pay includes variable components, which can both accommodate fluctuations in business results and in individual or team achievements, and reflect the level of pay in the business as a whole. Another important aspect is that variable forms of payment are generally linked to specific objectives. This represents a significant and efficient means of underlining and communicating business priorities.

It is one thing to send round a communiqué to inform all employees or all managers that the business objective for this year is to make profit X and to increase turnover by Y; it is quite another to notify them that the year's bonus of Z per cent depends upon whether or not these aims are achieved. The English say 'put your money where your mouth is', and this seems very appropriate here.

There are also forms of reward that have an *indirect monetary value*. These include, for example, systems offering share options. These offer only potential and not guaranteed reward. It is the nature of such systems that any return is deferred and often conditional. The emphasis often ultimately lies more on longer-term ownership than on definitive and immediately disposable cash values. Financial participation and share options will be discussed in a separate chapter.

A pension and insurance system that is the business's own or is specific to the firm is the purest form of reward that has deferred and indirect monetary value. Such systems can be seen as part of the reward only to the extent that they are financed by the business.

Other indirect monetary value rewards are expense accounts and free travel, but here too only to the extent that they go beyond the demands of the business and the usual functions of the job. Among other perquisites are company cars, loan guarantees and a host of others services provided by the business, some more popular and substantial than others.

Efficiency of the Reward Components

The question of the effect of reward can be approached from two directions:

1. How efficient is reward in satisfying individual needs?
2. What contribution does reward make to achieving the business objectives?

For the most part it can be asserted that the first consideration influences the second.

CONSIDERATION 1: REWARD AND INDIVIDUAL NEED

It is common knowledge that different people have different needs, so no one system can be expected to cover the huge variety of needs. In order to come as close as possible to this goal, attempts have been made to put together the pay package in such a way that it incorporates all the latest and most attractive elements. This has led to most businesses having very similar systems: a thoroughly logical consequence of the common practice of benchmarking.

The components of the pay package have dramatically altered over the course of time. While just 20 years ago, at least in Europe, talk of bonuses and variable pay for management and qualified specialists was unheard of, the exact opposite is true today. Salaries were once fixed and in due course raised at certain intervals, and the increases never depended on performance alone, but much more on seniority. Today this practice would have a completely counterproductive effect, but at that time it did not in any way seem as inappropriate as it does now. It must be remembered that the two main criteria for reward in those times were responsibility and experience. Performance was understood to be a natural or necessary product of these factors and was the basic precondition for employment and promotion. The only exception to these incremental increases was when someone moved to a different employer, especially in qualified professions and in jobs requiring leadership responsibility: from at least the level of the skilled worker, foreman or the head of department upwards.

Since then the main focus of reward strategies has been subject to unremitting change. Age or length of service are no longer relevant to determining pay, whose level is increasingly driven by the market. Thus more and more detailed comparisons are made so that businesses are able to ensure that their level of reward remains competitive in the struggle for talent and ability.

This attentiveness to the market makes a flexible pay scale necessary. Strict limits or ranges are no longer viable. Nor can a slow incremental growth from a starting salary to a maximum reflecting experience and years of service be reconciled with market and performance orientation.

Differentiating the level of pay in a business is sensibly achieved by considering:

- market price
- contribution made by the job (ranging from long-term strategic roles to short-term operational roles), which equates to level of responsibility
- individual performance
- results achieved (both the business results as well as individual goals)
- development potential.

Forming the aforementioned reward components and differentiating for individual needs are both contingent upon these criteria. It is thus likely that the expectations of the overwhelming majority of actual and potential workers can be met. By using the occasional employee questionnaire it is also possible to measure the degree of satisfaction: note *satisfaction*, not *motivation*, for it can be assumed that reward is a means to avoid dissatisfaction or create satisfaction, but that is a long way from motivation. Satisfaction with the level and type of reward or, in short, with the pay, is desirable, but it goes no further. This satisfaction does not extend to other aspects of the work and it certainly does not compensate for shortcomings in other areas.

Important as pay is, motivation is generated from other sources, as demonstrated in the section entitled 'Motivation'.

There is a – little used – possibility to go a step further than offering the latest and most attractive, but nevertheless standardized pay package: different combinations of components can be offered according to individual needs and be correspondingly varied.

An example of this is the aptly named *cafeteria-system*. Employees can choose from the available pay package what and how much of each component they want. Each these reward elements is priced. The possible options are restricted by the overall cost limits that are prescribed for every individual.

This method aims to maximize the benefit produced in return for particular, fixed costs. A tailor-made package can be selected according to the individual's circumstances, family life, individual priorities and preferences. If these circumstances and priorities change, the package can be amended. Where one person might subordinate a wage increase to a guaranteed loan through the firm at a favourable rate of interest, another in turn might prefer to receive substantial share options rather than a cash bonus, or vice versa.

In practice cafeteria systems are not used very often. They take a great deal of effort to implement, and the way each component of the reward is priced can cause difficulty and controversy. It is therefore seldom encountered and then only in a rather modest form with a limited range of options. It is most often found where the overall reward is put together from a number of assorted components, of which many are offered in kind and fewer in cash, mainly because this has various tax benefits. This is rarely the case in Europe or North America.

Where reward consists mainly of money, there is less opportunity for selection on a cafeteria basis. Money remains the most functional of goods, enabling people who draw it out of the bank and use it to decide for themselves what they can get, rather than what they can be given.

CONSIDERATION 2: REWARDS AND BUSINESS OBJECTIVES

Let us turn now to the second question, namely how efficient the components of reward are with respect to business objectives.

The surest method of creating an effective correlation here is to show as clearly as possible how the business objectives accord with aims targeted by the various components of reward. Thus the reward will provide an incentive to achieve the relevant objectives. This complex will be discussed in greater detail in the chapter on incentives. However, incentives are not everything, and in particular they are far from being motivation, although they have often been regarded as such. This point has already been made more than once in other contexts. Within the boundaries of the incentive to perform, reward systems can contribute to fulfilling business objectives; their contribution is not that impressive, however.

Chao C. Chen *et al.* published an interesting analysis based on research conducted in the United States under the title 'Do Rewards Benefit the Organization?' The study concluded that *intrinsic rewards* (in the form of interesting tasks, creative freedom and the like, see below) combined with salary increases would have a better effect for the business than individual financial premiums or bonuses.

The starting point was that reward systems have a beneficial effect. This was in turn traced to the assumption that organizations pay people for behaving in a way that is of service to the organization. It was discovered, however, that the supposed link between motivation, performance and pay could not be unconditionally accepted. Three reasons were offered to explain this.

- The way the individual behaves on the day, while aiming to achieve a bonus, is not always advantageous to the organization.
- Different forms of reward have different capacities to stimulate people and to serve the organization. For example, rewards subject to externally imposed controls can have a thoroughly restrictive effect on performance, especially in innovative work that needs high qualifications.
- Establishing the effectiveness of a financial reward for the organization is a very vague and subjective affair.

Intrinsic rewards were found to have the most positive effect for the organization. These include, for example, challenging tasks, working with competent colleagues, an intellectually stimulating climate, the opportunity to develop new initiatives, and the chance to pursue one's own ideas. In contrast, extrinsic rewards, such as variable pay, proved much less effective.

The outcome of this analysis is not surprising, for it reflects the difference between continuous motivation and superficial and *ad hoc* incentives.

The Emergence of Global Reward Strategies

Since the mid-1980s there has been a noticeable trend towards worldwide convergence in reward strategies, which has been dominated by the United States. In Europe this influence was first observable in the United Kingdom and later continued its march eastwards and southwards. The North American influence is also stamped upon Latin America.

A significant characteristic of North American reward strategy is the high proportion of short and long-term incentives. The latter mostly include an element of shares.

In Europe the emphasis on incentives has recently grown to a remarkable degree, although it has not reached the same extent as in the United States, for there are hardly any notable long-term incentive strategies (in the United Kingdom, however, things run a little differently). Share systems are used more as a mark of esteem and to emphasize the feeling of togetherness, and less as a direct incentive system. Although the financial advantages from shares can be truly considerable, they are often associated with less complex conditions than in the United States.

The typical pay package in the American recipe, especially for the middle and upper management levels, caters for a clearly materialistic and also mobile society, where individual businesses express their own culture and moral concepts strongly. In effect, they invite their employees to accept and participate, and if these concepts are rejected there is an equally unequivocal demand to leave voluntarily.

It is difficult to prove that true variability exists in the US incentives. In general, even poor performances or results still allow room for some form of pay-out or even pay increases. From time to time the parameters will be modified here and there. It must be remembered, however, that America is a clear example of what might be called the market-performance paradox.

If a high proportion of the variable reward components for a manager or a job depend primarily upon performance and results, then when the results are poor the overall reward can fall very dramatically below the usual market value. In such a situation, unless businesses want to run the risk of losing people from key positions, they will for better or for worse have to be prepared to compromise on the bonuses, perhaps reducing them, but not allowing them to fall entirely by the wayside.

If there is a link at all between the levels of performance and reward, then it is only a weak one. Despite, or perhaps even because of this, there is almost everywhere in Europe a growing trend to practise this kind of incentive system, even though in some areas the economic situation occasionally seems to run contrary to this trend.

The 'three-thirds' policy applied frequently for upper management in the United States can illustrate the significance of variable reward. The three 'thirds' are basic salary, short-term bonus and long-term bonus. The variable component thus comprises over 60 per cent of the package. In the United Kingdom, in contrast, it makes up about 40–50 per cent of the pay packet for the upper management levels, while in Germany, the Netherlands, Belgium and France it is generally around 30–40 per cent. Further East and South the proportion decreases in comparison.

In most Asian and Pacific countries the differences in reward between the various management levels are much less than in North America and Western Europe. In Japan, for example, the income of a chief executive is about 32 times higher than the average worker's wage. That may sound a lot, but it is minimal compared to the 150 times more found in the United States. Generally, pay in less 'Western' cultures is much more closely linked to age and length of service, leading to a certain standardization. There is a tendency to avoid accentuated differentiation between individuals. Pay and the occasional bonus for distinguished service are more strongly dependent upon the say and judgement of the superior than on systems and formulas. In many African countries perquisites are more important than cash payments.

International (regional) management markets and reward structures seem to be developing in the 'Western world' at least, and to a certain extent in parts of Asia. It is anticipated that over the course of time businesses will develop international payment strategies for international (and professional and executive) management positions, and thus partly withdraw from the traditional reward structures of their countries.

> In short, it can be asserted that the globalization of reward strategies represents in the main an Americanization. That is in itself neither good, bad or indifferent. The crucial factor is how it is implemented, not what it is called.

Future Developments

In a world of global markets and growing global competition, and an almost proverbial 'war for management talent', the significance of reward strategies is increasing. In the new world of international competition among a declining number of ever more powerful players, in a world of increasingly rapid innovation, where rivals can emulate any competitive advantage relating to technology, finance or the market within months and not years, then first and foremost the skills and abilities of the management and the quality of the employees will afford the business a lasting competitive edge.

That particularly applies to the New Economy, for only a few people will be able to achieve lasting business success through good economic management by assessing and accepting the following challenges:

- innovation
- dexterity at turning ideas into actions
- entrepreneurial risk
- enthusiasm and emotion
- the wide gap between an actual situation and future hopes
- new, untried technologies and techniques
- great opportunities and equally great dangers.

These – relatively few – people are in such high demand that no reward is too high for businesses to offer them.

Under the impetus of an ever-increasing rate of change, there is a steady movement away from a perhaps logical but in practice unrealistic belief in a causal chain from the business policy to the reward policy. The success of these policies has always been somewhat questionable. The different components move in extremely varied temporal dimensions and are subject to highly fluctuating environmental influences. When there is good reason to change the reward strategy, it does not mean that the entire personnel policy or even the business policy has to be changed too. On the contrary, there is often an attempt to achieve a certain stability and continuity by changing as little as possible.

> In future more frequent renovation of reward strategies will be more important than – all too often unsuccessful – efforts to keep them consistent. In a world of 'fun' and 'novelty', change and renewal are in themselves valuable qualities.

The traditional notions of reward continue to ask a little too much from a mechanistic relationship of cause and effect. Every component of the pay package is expected to trigger or direct certain behaviour. This has led to a proliferation of reward based on merit, short and long-term payment systems, shareholding plans, options, profit sharing, 'gainsharing', incentives, deferred pay and other methods. It is almost as if each of the various components of reward can trigger different behaviour at the touch of a button: this button for short-term success, that one for longer-term success; this one for growth, that one for staff development and so on. However, behaviour is not normally differentiated in this way. Excessive specialization is generally characterized more by complexity than by effectiveness.

> Pay must be immediately comprehensible, with transparent criteria for performance. Exceptional performance should be rewarded exceptionally, and indeed promptly. Rewarding performance should mainly relate to the achievement of medium-term strategic goals. One, at the most two, components of reward should suffice. Confusion and conflict between short and long-term aims, performance, results and potential must be avoided.
>
> More than ever before it will be necessary to discern between fads and fundamentals.

Successful reward strategies limit themselves to two or three main aims: decent pay for all employees of the core business area and top pay for the stars. For the uppermost management levels there should be the possibility of an additional bonus that depends upon the achievement of medium-term strategic goals as well as the growth of the business.

The significant differences in the level of reward that still exist between individual countries will gradually be levelled out as a consequence of growing mobility in a shrinking economic world. This development is already beginning to surface in senior management positions in international companies and will undoubtedly continue as greater transparency and ease of comparability unfold. They stem from the fact that rewards for leading and key positions are already often denominated in US dollars, as well as the fact that Euros are now in daily use in most European countries and very much so also in candidate states in Eastern Europe.

- A major simplification of reward systems is desirable.
- It will inevitably be acknowledged that complexity confuses more than it stimulates.
- Reward strategies will simplify, but not neglect, financial and extrinsic elements; pay is very important, especially in terms of the level of pay and transparency about how it has been determined.
- The intrinsic elements, that is, the components of reward based on the individual, tasks and development, will be fashioned with much more vigour and be made much more effective than they are now. It is by no means an entirely new insight that few people join a business because of pay alone, and even less is pay guaranteed to have a prolonged, continued and motivating effect.

- Few people leave a business solely because of pay, even though superficially this may often appear to be the case.
- We would be well advised to foster the motivational, socio-economic function of rewards.

A New Reward Model

In the light of what has been described above, it is recommended that rewards based on money or monetary value should be substantially simplified. This yields three main elements:

- fixed pay
- variable pay
- pension provision.

ELEMENT 1. FIXED PAY

The greater part of income should consist of an element that has been fixed for a lengthy period of at least a year. This should be expressed as the annual salary. The annual salary is not, however, paid everywhere in 12 equal monthly instalments; it may come in 13 or 14 instalments, depending on local custom, and it sometimes also includes additional forms of service. The annual salary as a standard value balances out these differences and, in contrast to a monthly figure, represents the complete value of the income. This not only makes comparisons between businesses easier, but also between countries. The use of the Euro and US dollar as statutory or optional denominations for income further increases transparency.

The fixed part of the reward (salary) should make up two-thirds of the overall pay, which is made up of both fixed and variable components (since pension provision is a deferred reward it will not be considered here). In senior positions the fixed proportion may be less, and in lower level jobs it may be more. This reflects long established practice and is also logical. Higher positions receive correspondingly higher incomes, so even a relatively low proportion of pay more than covers the cost of living. The variable part can accordingly be higher, reflecting the fact that higher positions have a greater influence on results.

Within a business the scales within which wages and salaries move are differentiated according to variations in the level of responsibility. A long time ago the level of responsibility was simply derived from the hierarchical position and perhaps from the job description. Later, analytical methods of assessing the content of the job were used to make a finer distinction between different positions, which may have enjoyed the same hierarchical level but were nevertheless very different in significance. The result was often 15, 20 or more job classifications, and each was allotted its own pay scale. In today's flatter organization structures there will be six, eight, or at the most ten categories, even in large businesses.

The traditional pay scales were broad, with sometimes a difference of 100 per cent between the lowest and highest points for a particular grade. Hence it could take a long time to journey up the scale. In a time in which not only the half-life of knowledge, but also the benefit of experience is dramatically declining, broad pay scales make little sense. Indeed, they conflict with the reality of the frequent change of jobs, both within a business and between businesses.

There should be a concerted attempt to keep pay scales tight to reflect today's demands: for example, 90 as an entrance value, 100 as a normal value and 110 as the maximum. 100 should be the designated 'market value' for the relevant job or type of work. Such market values are continuously being readjusted in the light of countless studies offered by remuneration consultants. Larger businesses, or businesses offering jobs that are harder to compare, can bring consultants in to help or conduct tailor-made comparisons themselves. Annually, or perhaps at slightly longer intervals, market values are brought up to date, which generally means they are raised.

The incremental system within these scales is simple and easy to understand: at the outset the salary is 90; after one or two years it should reach 100. Should that not be the case, then there are clear shortcomings demanding decisive action to rectify them, otherwise there will be a question mark over the person's continued employment in that particular position or perhaps even in the business. 110 should be achieved by someone demonstrating especially high performance and high potential (perhaps the values on the potential and performance graph on page 99 are still fresh in the memory).

Salary (the fixed cost) thus expresses:

- responsibility
- market value
- performance and potential

This requires no complicated process or lengthy administrative procedure.

ELEMENT 2. VARIABLE PAY

About a third of the overall pay – in leading positions a little more, in lower positions a little less – should take the form of an incentive/bonus. The exact percentage depends on the extent to which the targets, which were set to achieve certain results, were actually met. These targets are generally defined in terms of a threshold value, below which no bonus is granted, and a maximum value, the surpassing of which does not result in higher bonuses. There is no need to go into further detail here, as later an entire chapter is devoted to incentives.

It is recommended that two objectives are set as the basis for the bonus: first, profit (pre-tax; or another more common value in the business accounts), and second, increase in turnover. Both objectives are set on a yearly basis. The target for growth, however, normally has significance over more than one year and is therefore to be viewed as a medium-term criterion. It is on the whole prudent not to set targets for profit and growth for the whole business, but from the middle management upwards and only for the divisions concerned with the relevant tasks.

Where it is legally, structurally and administratively possible and sensible, half of the bonus should be granted in cash and the other half in shares or other schemes of joint ownership. These shares or schemes should be subject to a minimum term of retention (for example five years). This will strengthen the bonds with the business and generate a greater financial interest in its long-term success. Share options will be discussed thoroughly in a later section.

In this way, efforts and costs will be kept to a minimum while the greatest possible transparency will be achieved. Moreover, an effective stimulus in both the short and long term will be generated, supporting the main aims of the business, which normally centre around profitability and growth.

ELEMENT 3. PENSION PROVISION

In the twentieth century the main pillar to support provision for the elderly took the form of a state pension. Recently however this single-pillar tradition has been called into question. Whereas in the past a second or third pillar in the form of a company pension or private savings formed only a minor, if useful, supplement to state support, chiefly for those who had higher disposable incomes, a three-pillar system that relies on all these provisions is becoming more prevalent.

To avoid going into excessive detail, which would be incongruous here, only the company pension provision will be discussed, and then only in general terms.

The measures taken by a business to contribute to the pension scheme of its employees belong in the category of reward. More exactly, the pension is a deferred reward, because a business's current payments into the scheme will only benefit its employees later. The most sensible arrangement seems to be a pension provision in the form of a company or industry-wide pension fund. The business and the employee normally both pay contributions to this fund, and the pension is paid out upon retirement. The amount is determined by the contributions and by actuarial calculations based on economic conditions and stipulations of the pension fund. Pension funds are subject to precise legal regulations and controls over how they are managed and the nature of the contributions.

There are basically two main forms of company pension schemes. In the first, contributions are defined and pension payments are based on the yield harvested by investing the contributions. Thus it is not possible to foresee exactly how much a pension will be, but there can also be no shortfall or surplus in the contributions.

In the second type, the amount of the pension is defined largely according to the salary or wage level and years of service to the company. The contributions are calculated to achieve the planned level of pensions. Contributions compared with pension payments may cover costs exactly, or there may be a shortfall or a surplus.

Company pension provision is not a recent invention. In the past it was traditionally more like a voluntary fringe benefit. Often only the company made any contribution. The pension reserves were mostly held as reserves in the business's accounts and were not transferred to an autonomous pension fund. Payments from the company pension scheme were in general reserved for those who remained in the business until they retired.

Over the course of time pension regulations became more and more established; pension provision often became a legal entitlement and ultimately achieved independence in the form of the pension fund. Business contributions are costs comparable to other reward costs. The contributions made by the future pensioner represent a form of saving to secure an income in later life.

Since it is no longer the case, as it was so often earlier, that a large part of someone's working life is spent in one business, the question increasingly arises as to whether pension entitlements should be transferable. Because mobility is demanded, desired and practised, it makes sense that employees should be able to retain or take their pension entitlements with them. This is becoming a growing consideration not only within the borders of individual countries, but also across them. Policy and legislation are required here, both at the level of the nation state, and at the level of international agreements or of the European Union.

At this point we will end the discussion of company pensions as deferred rewards. This discussion has of course been by no means exhaustive, but has deliberately selected only those aspects that tie in with the theme of reward.

OTHER SUPPLEMENTARY BENEFITS

In many businesses a much greater number of components of reward will undoubtedly be found than the three suggested here. The wide variety of supplementary services and fringe benefits offered by many businesses have a long history and cannot be changed easily. However, it never does any harm to conduct the occasional study with an aim to reform the pay packet and make it less complex and more transparent.

It is basically advisable to limit the main components to three, as this allows the most important goals of a reward strategy to be achieved efficiently. It may be sensible to include other elements when the tax benefits then gained by the employees are greater than the benefits they would receive if the equivalent sums were given as extra rewards in salaries. Another reason for offering such reward elements could be the 'market': if it is customary to attach special benefits to particular jobs, then these can hardly be dropped without making it difficult to recruit the most suitable people for those posts.

CHAPTER 6

Incentives

Bonus, Incentive Systems, Result-related Pay

Variable Pay

Variable pay is playing an ever increasing role within the overall pay package, especially at management level and for qualified employees. For a long time US organizations have been the front-runners. Here, particularly in top management, two-thirds of the annual income typically consists of variable elements: short-term incentives (annual bonus), longer-term bonus programmes (from three to five years) and stock options (see pages 151–6).

> Today the general rule is: the higher the management position and the more highly qualified the task, the greater the proportion of the variable pay.

It has not always been this way. Originally, variable reward was conceived specifically for simple, repetitive, manual work. Frederick Winslow Taylor, whom we have already met in the discussion on motivation, recommended in his 1911 publication *Principles of Scientific Management* that every factory worker should be prescribed an accurately analysed, restricted and measurable working tempo, regulated by time limits. Keeping within the limits should result in a premium being paid.

For a long time, piecework rates, hourly rates and sales commissions were recognized incentive systems that aimed to stimulate and reward improved performance. They were unquestionably successful and are still applied today, albeit now not to the same extent. In the past, one of the characteristics of qualified employment and of work in higher positions was a fixed salary, not variable components of reward. The clerical white-collar workers were clearly elevated above the labouring blue-collar workers in terms of reward, employment law and social standing. In a sense the beliefs of that time seemed to influence the fact that McGregor's Theory

X was applied to the 'labourers' and Theory Y to the 'clerks' (see section on 'Motivation').

With the growing Americanization of global reward strategies since the 1980s, variable pay has gained increasing importance in leading and key positions in Europe too. This of course is now not about piecework or hourly premiums or sales commissions.

> The logic of the new form of variable pay concerns both the incentive to succeed and participation in success.

The so-called *short-term incentives* are the most frequently used. This entails making the promise of a reward conditional upon the objectives for a business year. The reward varies depending on whether the predetermined objectives have been achieved, surpassed or not met. The reward is in the main calculated as a percentage of the basic salary and then paid. Every year the variable reward (the 'bonus') must be earned anew.

In order to strike a balance with the short-term orientation of the annual bonus, *longer-term incentives* were also developed. These are based on business objectives for a period of generally three to five years. Stock/share options, which are examined in a separate chapter, count among the longer-term incentives.

Incentive is not Automatically Motivation

At the end of the chapter on motivation it was argued that motivation and incentive cannot be lumped together. Motivation is all-embracing, thus encompassing the motivation to work, and concerns innate, acquired and learnt needs. It also incorporates the desire to even out dissonances and reach agreements (for example in what a person contributes and receives in return); hence it determines basic positions, helps people to discover what they are striving for and defines goals.

The fundamental willingness to work hinges on motivation. Motivation influences the choice of job or career type; it determines the personal value placed on work and success in the career; it governs the level of ambition; it is also responsible for a greater or a lesser need for power, for a desire to please others or for indifference towards them.

It has been demonstrated that it is impossible not to be motivated: there is constant inducement from motives and influence from desires to give direction to our lives and thus also to our work.

> Motivation can be likened to an engine, which moves our vehicle along the career and work path with more or less force, more or less speed and more or less energy.
>
> 'Incentives' are the fuel, the accelerator pedal, the steering wheel, which can change the tempo and the direction in the short term; they can even be the brakes, bringing everything to a halt (for not all incentives provide an effective and guaranteed impetus).

When motivation and incentive are used synonymously, both are miscon-strued: motivation is trivialized and the demands on incentives placed too high. Incentives are, however, very important, for many tasks and require-ments at work are accomplished more effectively and quickly through the impetus generated by incentives than if there were no incentives at all.

Incentives: What they Can and Cannot Do

As we have just argued, incentives cannot replace motivation. When the fundamental motivation to work is lacking, then the organization of the tasks, the objectives and the rewards, all of which aim to stimulate, will have only a very weak effect.

Nor can an incentive in the form of a promised bonus payment or salary increase compensate for a lack of interest in the task, too little challenge, too much routine or lack of development opportunities. There are occa-sional attempts to 'motivate' through higher pay. This never achieves its aim. It is of course pleasant to receive more money, but this pleasure does not lead to motivation (those who have read the chapter on motivation will be reminded here of Herzberg and the 'hygiene factors'). Experience tells us that the good feelings caused by a wage rise or a bonus payment are amazingly short-lived. After swiftly becoming accustomed to the bonus, people will soon expect it every time, and their needs will rapidly adapt to the increased means that they have at their disposal.

> Incentives can, however, build upon existing motivation extremely effectively and thus induce high performance and good results.

Incentives – above all financial incentives – can thus result in the phenom-enon mentioned in the last paragraph of people becoming accustomed to a higher or an additional income. Once granted, the higher salary or bonus will soon be seen as the norm. Therefore the possibility of earning a further increase or a further bonus has an additional effect, inasmuch as it serves as an incentive to put in the performance required for the increase or bonus.

Incentives are simple, crude but effective, and no fine tuning or complex cogitation can be expected: when a bonus is promised for boosting pre-tax profit by X, then perhaps not all, but certainly most people will want to achieve X. They would indeed like to earn the bonus. Money is key to this, but self-esteem, ambition, and the desire to perform and compete play a role. The promise of a bonus is crude as an incentive because it does not allow for any nuances. For example, when it is feared that X cannot be reached under prevailing market conditions, then reducing advertising expenses might lower the costs. That may secure X in the short term, but retribution will soon come in the form of a falling market share.

When the bonus aim is to increase turnover by Y and the achievement of this aim is in jeopardy, then there might be a temptation to lower prices. This will perhaps achieve Y, but the profits will be the leaner for it. In both cases the incentive has delivered what it had promised, but has also entailed unintended and negative side effects.

With full awareness of the possible consequences, objectives can be combined for the promise of a bonus: 'increasing profit by X while maintaining advertising costs', or 'increasing turnover by Y with a profit of Z'. This can be helpful, but it will not entirely rule out the possibility that other variables will be enlisted in order to achieve the bonus.

Systems adopting success-based variable pay constantly call upon objectives. Because of this they can very effectively communicate priorities and underline those business aims that must in all circumstances be achieved. When the aims have been identified and formulated, it should come as no surprise that every effort is made to achieve them.

This also hints at negative consequences: the promise of a bonus limits the interest of the people concerned to earning the bonus, whereby they might not always employ the best tactics. There is a desire to find the greatest possible safeguards against risks; even in terms of the objectives there is a tendency to take the safe option and to negotiate aims that can be achieved as easily as possible.

The promise of a bonus implies the threat of a punishment should the bonus not be achieved. An incentive is thus both stick and carrot at the same time and many will feel that it is psychological manipulation.

Because people do not want to miss the opportunity to earn a bonus, it stirs not exclusively negative but certainly frequently ambivalent feelings: there is the pleasing prospect of a bonus, but at the same time also the dispiriting prospect that the aims may be missed and the bonus therefore withheld. The risk of going home empty-handed is rightly or wrongly further heightened by the fear that the aims will be missed not through personal failure, but because of the inadequacy of a third party or because of unforeseeable and unavoidable circumstances. This gloomy picture is darkened even more by the previously mentioned *fundamental attribution error* ('*we* deserve the credit for every success; *the others* are to blame for any failure').

Despite everything, incentives can animate and encourage and retain this effect, even if side effects must be reckoned with.

Punished by Rewards is the thought-provoking title of a book by Alfie Kohn. He took the viewpoint that rewards and incentives are extremely problematical, arguing that they are severely manipulative, are used as a means of power and have at best a superficial effect. Their true nature is not understood as they are employed again and again: heads of management, teachers and parents can exercise their authority legitimately through the promise, granting or withholding of rewards. Because this – largely – results in desired changes in behaviour, reaction or results, they view rewards as effective.

Bonuses and salary increases are the management's means of control: gold stars, public praise, toys and sweets are the tools of power for the teacher. They will have no influence on the motivation of the employees, pupils or children, but have an immediate, albeit only superficial, effect. The logic of a very simple causal relationship dictates 'do that, then you will get this'. On the basis of his findings, Kohn called this *pop behaviourism*. His is an empirically-based argument, proposing that the causes of behaviour stretch far back into human history and probably started when people began to domesticate animals and learn new crafts, for which among other things rewards were crucial.

Kohn recalls the two main strands of the theory of learning, namely classical and instrumental conditioning. The first hinges upon certain influences or phenomena that elicit natural reactions. When these influences are combined with an artificial signal, the signal acts representatively and triggers the same reaction. The most common example is Pavlov's dog: a dog begins to salivate when it smells meat, which is a natural reaction. The dog can be 'trained' to salivate, even when there is no meat, if a bell is rung each time before the meat is produced. Ultimately the meat is omitted and only the bell rings; that is already sufficient to encourage salivation. The dog has learnt to associate meat with the signal from the bell.

The second form of learning is triggered by a stimulus coming *after* the action: when a reward follows certain behaviour, then this behaviour will be repeated in future. B. F. Skinner founded his theory of behavioural science upon this notion. Kohn criticizes the application of behaviourism to human behaviour. Behaviourists subsume people along with animals simplistically under the collective term 'organisms'. These organisms ultimately differentiate themselves through the type, and not the causes, of their behaviour. According to Kohn this is untenable and incorrect. He scathingly remarks: 'B. F. Skinner could be described as a man who conducted most of his experiments on rodents and pigeons and wrote most of his books about people.'

Kohn gives a series of examples in his criticism of the simple use of rewards to engender a change in behaviour. One describes how an American school tried to encourage the children to read books. Every time they could prove they had read a book, they received a pizza voucher. What happened? The children read the thinnest and shortest publications that could just about be classified as books, and then eagerly cashed in their pizza vouchers. The result, concludes Kohn, is overweight children who hate books.

Kohn is correct insofar as motivation and incentive are two separate entities. As far as incentives are concerned, however, there is a more optimistic aspect. This depends on being aware of what incentives can and cannot achieve, and on using them accordingly

Incentives in Practice

The application of incentives and pay based on results or success, especially for the management level and employees in key positions or with special qualifications, is not only practised in the United States and Europe, but is common throughout almost the entire world.

The extent of the variable reward is generally tending to rise. There does not appear to be a saturation point. It is known that money cannot guarantee happiness, although that seems to depend very much on the individual. On the macro-level, too, affluence seems unable to buy happiness outright. There are 'National Happiness Studies' that show there is hardly any

In the author's experience, which diverse income studies have also confirmed, there is a variable element in the overall pay packet of board members and managing directors in well over 90 per cent of all cases. The proportion fluctuates within a very broad scale of about 10 to 50 per cent of the fixed amount. In some rare cases it is even more.

This predominantly concerns short-term (limited to one year) incentives. Apart from share options, long-term incentives are seldom encountered outside North America.

relationship between the gross national product and national feelings of happiness or unhappiness.

With particular reference to the individual, it is known that money does not provide sustained motivation. It is, however, a powerful incentive, and its influence extends far beyond the need to provide a decent standard of living. There are several different reasons for this. Two main generally tenets apply. First, the intensity of the desire for money and profit increases according to the status attached to it. Second, the prospect of making more profit or earning more money leads immediately to the need to exploit that opportunity. Both observations are probably justifiable by behaviourist theories. They are grounded in the hunter/gatherer past and everybody can relate to them.

The 'rich' always want to be richer. Entrepreneurs, top managers, stars in the fields of sport, music or film, and other celebrities are in no way financially naive, otherwise they would not be what they are. They have earned money, they know that things are as they are, and they will not change simply because some perceive the search for riches as the source of evil and corruption. People who do not see it this way generally had no great interest in financial success – or indeed in any other type of demonstrable success – in the first place, and therefore they have developed entirely different ambitions for their life and career. For those who remain in the thick of the hunt, the pursuit continues, for hunters measure themselves by the size of their catch. Konrad Lorenz's teachings are also important here, that humans are the only creatures that continue hunting after they have provided for the immediate necessities of life.

The major companies in national economies, like many individuals, are directed and indeed programmed towards growth. To have achieved a certain result (profit, rise in share price, income) is no reason to sit back and relax. On the contrary it signals a challenge to achieve even more in the following year or quarter.

Incentive Bonus Systems: Four Examples

The essential features of incentive systems can usefully be illustrated with four examples; two are short term and two long term.

Short Term (on an Annual Basis)

EXAMPLE I

- *Bonus objectives:*
  a) Pre-tax profit.
  b) Personal objectives (maximum of three): these goals must represent priorities related to the job. They must be quantitatively or qualitatively measurable.
- *Extent of the bonus:*
  0–40 per cent of basic salary.
- *Fulfilling the objectives:*
  Objective a) must be at least 90 per cent fulfilled. No bonus is paid if this threshold is missed, regardless of whether other objectives have been fulfilled. If it is 90 per cent fulfilled, then the bonus is calculated as 5 per cent of the basic salary. If it is 100 per cent fulfilled the bonus is 10 per cent. If it is 110 per cent fulfilled the bonus is 20 per cent.
  Objective b) may or may not be fulfilled. It is of no consequence to what extent the objectives are under or overachieved. Provided that objective a) is at least 90 per cent fulfilled, the bonus for the three personal objectives can amount to a maximum of 20 per cent.
- *Participants:* Members of the board of directors and the next two subordinate levels.
- *Bonus recommendation:* By the immediate superior.
- *Decision/Statement:* Chairman of the board of directors.
- *Payment:* In February of the year following the bonus period.
- Should the employee leave the business, the bonus is forfeited.
- The bonus does not bear on any entitlements to a company pension.

EXAMPLE II

- *Bonus objectives:*
  a) Quantitative business objectives (maximum of two), for example pre-tax profit, size, increase in turnover.
  b) Personal objectives (maximum of three): must be directly linked to the annual business plan; can be clearly ascertained whether they are fulfilled or unfulfilled; degree of fulfilment is measurable.

- *Extent of the bonus:*
  Maximum of 50 per cent of the basic salary.
- *Fulfilling the objectives:*
  a When one or both of the business objectives are 120 per cent fulfilled, the bonus is calculated at 25 per cent of the basic salary (for two objectives each one is worth 12.5 per cent). At least 85 per cent must be attained, at which level the bonus is 5 per cent, (or 2.5 per cent per objective). The bonus is graduated for achievements of between 85 per cent and 120 per cent of the objectives.
  b) The bonus percentage that has been determined for the quantitative business objective also applies for the personal objectives, according to the following criteria: it is paid in full when the personal objectives have been fulfilled, and 75 per cent when the objectives have nearly been reached. When the personal objectives have been missed, then this part of the bonus is not paid. When there are different degrees of fulfilment for the individual personal objectives, then each objective will be calculated at a rate of one-third of the overall percentage available for personal objectives.
- *Participants:* Members of the board of directors and the lower levels.
- Other conditions as in Example I.

COMMENTARY

Incentive bonus plans are less about the mechanics, which – as the both examples demonstrate – are really very simple. More important are the achievements that the plans should encourage and the signals they send out. Successful and effective incentive plans should thus be embedded in the business culture and harmonized with the business strategy. Our two examples illustrate that principle.

Plan I is stricter. The barrier that must be overcome to achieve a bonus at all is higher than in Example II. In the first example at least the profit objective (or at least 90 per cent of it) must be achieved. Only then is there a bonus, even for personal objectives. Should at least 90 per cent not be fulfilled, then it makes no difference whether the personal objectives themselves are achieved.

Plan I sends off the following signals: profitability is our primary aim. For a bonus to be considered this aim at least must be achieved. Achieving the other objectives is also important and, should the profit objective be fulfilled, the other achievements raise the overall bonus. Nothing, however, can take the place of profit.

Plan II places an equal emphasis on the quantitative business objectives and the personal objectives. The signals are clearly different from those in

Plan I, reflecting more the philosophy: our reward consists of fixed and variable parts. The variable part should underline particularly vital priorities and correspondingly reward the achievement of these priorities. Each objective is earmarked its own bonus potential. The same weight is placed on achieving the results of the business (one or two objectives) as on the three personal objectives together. However, the result counts for more than individual personal objectives.

It is anticipated that Plan I will be more selective than Plan II. From the author's experience it is to be expected that, averaging out several years for Plan I, about 80 per cent of the participants will actually receive a bonus. With Plan II a figure of far more than 90 per cent can be anticipated. The difference is to be traced to the knock-out effect of the result-based objectives in Plan I.

Is one of the two systems better than the other? Only inasmuch as one may be more or less suited to the business culture and more or less suited to reinforcing the business strategy.

Longer Term (Several Years)

EXAMPLE I
- *Objective:* Achieving the annually determined pre-tax profit continuously over a period of three years.
- *Extent of the bonus:* 0–30 per cent per year.
- *Fulfilling the objectives:* At least 90 per cent of the profit objective, the norm is 100 per cent, and the maximum is 110 per cent (exceeding this has no further effect on the bonus).
- *Calculating the bonus:* If the objective has been 90 per cent fulfilled, every participant will receive a 10 per cent bonus for each of the three years; with 100 per cent fulfilment 20 per cent will be credited, and with 110 per cent or more 30 per cent will be credited. If the 90 per cent target has not been achieved in one of the years, no bonus is credited.
- Payment is due after the end of the third year.
- Other conditions as with the short-term plans.

COMMENTARY
This is a very simple model, for the bonus calculation depends upon actually verifiable results from three consecutive years. The message is very clear: whoever achieves the business objectives each year has thus contributed to the long-term success and will be specially rewarded for it. This model does not use personal long-term plans as the basis of the bonus.

EXAMPLE II

- *Objective:* Achieving the cumulative profit objectives as well as the increase in turnover determined in the long-term (four-year) plan.
- *Extent of the bonus:* 0–30 per cent.
- *Fulfilling the objectives:* 90, 100 and 110 per cent as above.
- *Calculating the bonus:* Fulfilling the objectives of profit and turnover will be determined separately. Each objective fulfilled by 90 per cent earns a bonus of 5 per cent, for every 100 per cent fulfilled objective 10 per cent, and for every 110 per cent fulfilled objective 15 per cent.
- *Cycle:* Every second year a new four-year plan is drawn up. This initiates a new cycle for the bonus plan each time. That signifies the end of one four-year plan every second year, whereupon the bonus is accordingly paid. At this moment the cycles partly overlap one other.

COMMENTARY

Example II is a more 'full-blooded' form of longer-term incentive, linking in with the longer-term plans of the business. This affords it a discernable logic. In Example I, whether a bonus had been earned through the continuous-result-based objectives was determined in hindsight. In Example II, however, the incentive is to fulfil specifically determined plans for the future.

This alternative has, however, some complications: these are not so much a consequence of the cycles overlapping, but largely concern the suitability of the length of a four-year plan. This is certainly a long period, during which many unpredictable changes can arise, making the originally determined aims partly or completely irrelevant. Even if the plan is redrafted every two years, it is not easy to carry out the necessary adaptations, which however are vital to maintain both the level of incentive and the credibility of the way the bonus is calculated.

To conclude this set of examples of short and long-term incentive bonus plans, we should note the fact that it is not always advisable simply to buy programmes 'off the peg'.

Bonus plans should be as tailor-made as possible, particularly in terms of objectives, signals and requirements, though to some extent also in the mechanics of calculating bonuses. Such plans help to ensure that tasks will be performed according to the strategy and culture of the business.

Target setting

> Target setting is more than an integral part of incentive systems. It is the essential prerequisite for the efficiency of these systems.

- *Agreeing upon the short and long-term goals, as expressed in the business plan:* The incentive objectives will be identical to the business objectives for the first and perhaps also the second level of management. Where there is a high degree of specification in particular areas of the business or in particular jobs and their corresponding tasks, priorities and responsibilities, it is prudent to define tailor-made objectives. These, however, should always be derived from the larger business objectives.
- *Target agreement:* It is well known that genuine commitment to a goal cannot be authoritatively imposed from above, but exists only when there is agreement over the type and extent of the goal.

  A further reason for setting targets through agreement rather than decree is that, although targets that have been determined by senior management may well represent the strategic direction of the business and generally define a consistent 'top-down' approach, a certain amount of fine-tuning is sensible in actually implementing the targets in the departments. This can accommodate their more precise knowledge of specific details, local markets and suchlike in a 'bottom-up' fashion.
- *Measuring and fulfilling the goals:* It is essential that in the final analysis it can be assessed whether the objectives have been achieved, surpassed or failed. Objectively verifiable quantities prove most useful here. The assessment should not rely only on a quantitative scale, for there are also qualitative criteria. It is necessary, however, to define them clearly. Ideally this should have already been undertaken when the objectives were agreed upon. This will thus ensure absolute clarity about what should be achieved and how success is to be measured.

Essentially three categories of objectives are practical for incentive systems:

- *Financial objectives for the business:* For example pre-tax profit; results before interest, tax and write-offs and suchlike. Setting targets as incentives that are different from the main elements used in the business accounts should be avoided. That would not only lead to unnecessary duplication, but also blur the very important connection between performance and business results.

- *Other business objectives:* These may include increase in turnover, share of the market, and product innovation.
- *Personal objectives:* Such objectives are specifically tailor-made for individuals, their tasks and the contribution anticipated within a certain period. These objectives frequently focus upon priorities that lie outside the normal remit of the job. Often these objectives offer the opportunity to work on certain projects or with a team drawn together for a special task. It is especially important to personal objectives that the way in which performance is to be measured has been clearly discussed and determined in advance.

The examples of incentive plans above demonstrate that one should not set too many objectives. Two business objectives (one of which is financial) and two or three personal objectives allow for concentration upon the most important priorities. Whether or not each of these objectives is achieved has a crucial effect on the amount of the bonus. Should there be a long list of objectives, each one seeming completely reasonable, then the individual significance of each one might become so diluted that there is barely any incentive to fulfil it.

It is often sensible to place different emphases on the objectives. When there are three objectives, then each one may determine a third of the bonus potential. It can also be decided that a certain, especially important objective should determine half and each of the others a quarter of the bonus, or some other weighting selected to reflect the relevant significance of each objective. It is certainly not recommended that too little significance is attached to objectives. Going under a tenth of the proportion of the overall bonus potential is not advisable. Ultimately objectives and the financial incentives bound up with them should denote priorities and not trivialities.

CHAPTER 7

Financial Participation

Background

The idea of employees sharing in the business's success is not entirely new. In the 1930s at least – and perhaps even earlier – there was evidence of profit sharing. In the 1950s in Germany and other countries there were many noteworthy models of employee participation, both in the profit and in the equity of the business.

Interestingly, there was at the time – at least in Europe – little talk of financial participation at management levels. This may, among other reasons, have been because at this time there were still many more privately owned and family owned businesses, and therefore 'sharing' was already an essence of these concerns.

In the 1960s in the United States, especially at the top management level, profit sharing was already widely practised both in the form of profit-related incentives and in the form of stock options. In the early 1980s in the United Kingdom under the government of Margaret Thatcher, the instrument of share options was not only promoted (*share options* is the British expression, *stock options* the American) as a means of stimulating the entrepreneurial spirit, but also made more attractive through tax incentives. There was subsequently a similar occurrence with *profit-related pay*. For a long time businesses in France have been legally obliged under certain conditions to involve the employees in the profit (*participation*) or in the equity (*intéressement*). Similar models were also developed in other countries, for example in Sweden.

In 1991 and 1996 the European Commission published a comprehensive analysis under the acronym PEPPER: Promotion of Participation by Employed Persons in Profits and Enterprise Results (including equity participation) in member states. The aim of this publication was to examine the measures taken by the governments of the EU states to promote employee participation, and at the same time to encourage more developments in this direction.

Development

As far as the practice of financial participation is concerned (in whatever form it may take), it is still most prevalent in North America: for example variable (result-related) pay determined in the form of short, medium and also long-term bonus systems; employee stock options; and executive stock options.

This practice has disseminated from North America to South America, through the United Kingdom to Europe, and to a growing extent also towards Asia. The first agents of this practice were largely subsidiaries of American multinational companies, which created a market through 'imports' from their motherland. Gradually other companies entered or had to enter this market in order to remain competitive in the hunt for qualified employees.

The author led a study in 1998 and 1999 of more than 40 of the largest European companies. It indicated that the predominant majority practised one or several forms of employee participation. Share-option schemes made up the largest proportion, followed by profit-share schemes.

Almost all large companies offer their managements share options (so long as they are listed on the stock exchange as, bar a few exceptions, they all are).

Profit Sharing

This point will only be briefly touched upon. For one thing, profit sharing has already been discussed. Also, whether calculated by means of simple or complex formulae, traditional across-the-board profit sharing has far less incentive effect than individually designed bonus plans.

> The purpose of profit sharing is to awaken in the employees a greater interest in the economic situation of the business; to demonstrate clearly how fluctuations in business results bear on the share of the yield; to make employees aware of both the opportunities and the risks in the business world; to create a stronger bond with the business through sharing; and to increase the employees' interest in working efficiently and remaining competitive.

There have been decades of experience with different models of profit sharing. It can be asserted in hindsight that this did bring about some achievements. However, in most cases the effects are perhaps less capti-vating than was anticipated. The reasons for this have less to do with principle and more to do with practice:

- Because profit sharing is subject to fluctuations and payments may fall, it cannot comprise too large a proportion of pay, since a fall could endanger basic needs for subsistence. By taking proper precautionary measures, however, such effects can largely be absorbed.
- Even when profits have fallen, measures have sometimes been taken to keep the profit-sharing premiums artificially high. Where the results have been constant, however, people have begun to take such levels for granted; not to mention the fact that that these have sometimes been claimed – and indeed conceded – as acquired rights.
- It is often in practice difficult or inappropriate to explain fully how the share of the profit has been calculated. This might involve highly sensitive information, which for competitive reasons cannot easily be made public.
- Finally, and this is the most important point, in most businesses – unless they are very small and can be easily understood – employees cannot fathom how, when or whether they have clearly influenced the results as individuals or as a group. When measured against personal input, the yield of profit sharing can thus be unexpectedly high, but it can also be unexpectedly low.

Reviewing these considerations, one is struck by the question of whether similar assertions about employees' shares and share options will be made in hindsight in 5, 10 or 20 years. Even profit sharing was once excit-ing and sexy, although ultimately it fell victim to erosion through custom and unperformed or unperformable promises. That should be no cause for doubt or defeatism. However, something new will be needed again when the things we find interesting and refreshing today have passed their expiry date.

Equity Participation

Earlier known as 'co-ownership', equity participation has just as long a history as profit sharing. Until the 1950s it was predominantly based on models of a paternalistic nature. As these models were never very common, they were suited to originality and a pioneering spirit. At their core was a desire to overcome the socio-political gap between collectivism/communism and individualism/capitalism. In 1961 the author had the opportunity to examine the theories and different practices of the then predominant schemes of employee participation. It could be demonstrated in theory as well as in practice that the most telling motive for early models of participation was to create a form of internal business partnership.

Extending this glance into the past a little further, it is interesting to note that the *main advantages* of business co-ownership were perceived in the following effects:

- It developed of a sense of responsibility and self-esteem (thus was character-building).
- It reduced class divisions: ownership ceased to be a privilege and hence a watchword of the class struggle.
- As co-owners, workers developed a stronger bond to their company and its interests.
- Involvement had a stimulating effect on performance.
- People reduced current consumption in order to acquire private property (the key term is 'invested wage': the part of the wage put aside and invested in jointly-owned areas of the business).

There were also perceived disadvantages and objections; for example:

- In times of crisis, employees who had shares in the equity of the business that employed them ran the risk of losing not only their jobs but also their savings in one fell swoop.
- It could prove very difficult to realize part of the capital in co-ownership, especially when money was urgently needed.
- Even then administrative and legal problems often presented obstacles that were too difficult to overcome. In limited joint-stock companies the share could be realized relatively easily. This was also possible in limited partnerships, but for unlimited companies and private companies it proved very complicated indeed. Nevertheless, in practice there were a host of examples illustrating how these problems could be solved.

The situation that existed a few decades ago has been intentionally described a little more thoroughly and the contemporary terminology also retained. This illustrates how widespread and far-reaching have been the changes that have since taken place.

Social romanticism, the class struggle and ideologies are not as great an issue or as relevant as they used to be. Property is no longer a privilege of the few. Of course there are sufficient contrasts today: between young and old, native and foreigner, computer literate and illiterate, to name but a few – but these are different issues altogether.

If the talk today is of co-ownership or equity participation, then it mainly concerns the following reasons and objectives:

- Creating a common interest between the shareholders (owners), management and employees in raising the value of the business.
- Putting together a competitive pay packet.
- The incentive to perform.
- Newly founded businesses, which could otherwise offer only rather modest salaries, often use share options to attract highly qualified employees. In the 'New Economy' in particular some people became millionaires within a very short time; others in turn had their hopes dashed.

As already mentioned, equity participation is only practicable for joint-stock companies listed on the stock exchange. Employees can acquire shares basically through the following means:

- share options
- share-save schemes
- shares that are given away for free or can be acquired through a share purchase scheme.

As the most usual tool, *share options* will be discussed a little later in some detail.

In *share-save schemes* employees can allow a proportion of their wage or bonus to be put into a company saving scheme. After a certain time they are then entitled to buy company shares at a certain price. Employees may also use part of a bonus to purchase company shares immediately. As an additional incentive employees usually receive shares at a discount.

Occasionally businesses *give away shares* to the employees, for example to mark an anniversary of the company's foundation or a particularly good business year.

That all sounds much more simple than it is. It should be remembered that all these measures depend on the most varied of legal and tax requirements. The shareholders (general meeting) must also reach agreement on a number of points, including the use of share capital, the purchasing of the company's own shares or an increase in the number of shares. It would be taking on far too much to attempt to discuss all of the regulations, which also vary widely from country to country and are subject to change from time to time.

Matters of costs and communication should also be closely considered.

Costs

The costs of share options, share-save schemes and similar plans should not be underestimated. The expense goes beyond the setting-up and administrative running costs of the scheme. Costs are incurred because, in contrast to shares that are bought on the stock exchange, share options are generally given away free to the employees. Basically, to cover the costs of the obligation, a business can choose to purchase a corresponding number of their own shares as soon as they grant the share option, and put the shares on deposit until the option is exercised. Alternatively a business might choose to purchase the shares only when the share option is exercised. A third way to fulfil the option obligation is to issue new shares as and when needed. In proposing this course of action, one should be mindful of the 'dilution effect', which arises when the increase in the number of shares causes the *earnings per share* to decrease. Depending on the circumstances, different alternatives may be preferred or rejected out of hand, yet the costs will always be present. Ultimately share options represent an obligation that has to be honoured by the business.

One comment in passing: at the beginning of 2001 the economic press published reports about 'creative accounting' in the 'New Economy' of the United States. Among other things, it was reported that, to give the accounts a cosmetic balance, share options has been entered into the account books as 'free'. However, it turned out that both costs and obligations should properly have been entered into the books.

By the same token it was also reported that, due to the crash of share prices in many New Economy companies, payment by means of share options had ceased to function. If the current share price lies below the option price, which means that there would be no sense in exercising the option, then the options are said to be 'under water'. The employees then demand compensation, for example in considerably higher pay, for the fact that their income then remains at a relatively low level.

In order to measure the effort and calculate the costs of granting share options, the following factors need to be considered:

- Formulation of the strategy, objectives and the system.
- Legal and tax advice.
- Means of communication and time spent communicating.
- Advising the employees.
- Administrative running costs (internally incurred costs).
- Externally incurred costs (banks etc.).
- Costs of purchasing and keeping the company's own shares.
- Costs of releasing new shares (here it is important to take heed of the dilution of profit per share that was mentioned earlier).
- Stock-exchange risk. When the company's own shares are purchased as soon as the share options have been granted, the price may fall and that the business will have to write off the loss. When the shares are purchased only when the options are exercised, the shares have to be sold to the employee at a rate that lies below their market price.

In the author's experience the overall costs, including factoring in the potential costs (for example losses on the stock exchange), can amount to considerable sums, but substantially less than providing an identical benefit in cash payment.

Communication

This is also a very important point. As mentioned above, participation should achieve certain aims. However, these can hardly be achieved without detailed information about the essence of the participation and the mechanisms that support it.

If the expectation is that employees become shareholders, latching on to the notion of *shareholder value*, then it is not enough simply to grant them shares or options. Many might well have a rough idea of what shares are, that prices can rise and fall and that dividends can be paid. What options are, however, and how they function is less well known. These terms are often laden with the stigma of speculation, of being far too risky and unpredictable.

Transparency right from the start is an important precondition for success: employees who have shares and/or options are naturally (and quite justifiably) very interested in the development of the business, and indeed so they should be! Even more than the external shareholders, who may to a certain degree be 'professional', the employees need regular, clear and meaningful information to maintain their interest and to make them dedicated 'employee shareholders'.

Share Options

The principle of share options for employees is beautifully simple: the company grants – after taking legal and tax parameters into account – the employees in certain positions or on certain levels the right to acquire a predetermined number of company shares at some point in the future (for example after three or five years) at a predetermined price (such as the average price on the day the option is awarded). The rest is self-explanatory: the more substantial the rise in the share price, the greater the proceeds when the option is exercised (in this context 'exercise' means the employees declaring they want to take up the option). This will of course only be done if the share price has risen in the meantime.

An example as an illustration:

A business grants its employees in year X the option to purchase 100 company shares in year X+3 at a price of 10. In year X+3 the price is 15, so that if the option is exercised it will cost 1000 to acquire shares worth 1500.

The employee will therefore purchase the shares at the predetermined price. This is generally done through a bank commissioned to complete the transaction. The shares must now be purchased at the business's cost, unless the business purchased the shares when the option was granted and the shares are already in store. Occasionally new shares are issued to meet the option obligation (see above).

The employees then have various alternatives.

1. To keep shares thus acquired. Employees will retain the shares if they have enough money in hand to pay for them and they reckon on a further rise in the share price.
2. To sell the shares immediately and take the cash profit. There is then no risk of losing money in the future through gambling on the market price, but also no chance for further profit.
3. To sell only as many of the shares as is necessary to cover the cost of their acquisition. The remaining shares are kept (see point 1).

The reader's attention is drawn to the fact that, to maintain the focus of this book, no reference is made in this schematic outline to tax obligations or details of commission.

It is difficult to decide conclusively about the value of options. There are indeed methods to value them, which are yet to be discussed, but they are neither appropriate nor designed for reliably predicting future proceeds. The only certainty is that nothing can be lost by exercising an option; at worst nothing will be gained. This again leaves tax issues out of the equation: if a tax obligation arises as soon as the options are granted, then there is a risk that this tax will represent a loss to the employee should the share price fall or fail to rise.

Executive Share Options

The term 'share' rather than 'stock' will be used for the share options awarded in many businesses to managers, experts, especially qualified employees, people accomplishing exceptional achievements or others with particularly high potential.

The fundamental principles are the same as those described above. However, executive options differ in many respects from the simple form generally used in share options for employees in general (all-employee share options).

The first striking difference is the *scale of executive options*. There are of course no standardized norms for these and there are huge differences between businesses and countries. It is, however, not unusual for the value of an executive share option to equal or exceed by several times the annual salary (that is in terms of the value of the shares at the time of the options are awarded, which by definition has nothing to do with the potential profit).

It is noteworthy that for a lengthy period, in which there was really only a bull market and the bear market hardly ever figured, many had the impression that it was not a question of whether, but only of how much, profit would be made out of share options.

Executive share options are not only most widespread but also most diverse in the United States. The most extreme examples especially excite wonder and criticism, but in general the tool of share options is recognized as an efficient long-term incentive. A few years ago the United Shareholders' Association in Washington contracted the Harvard Business School to conduct an investigation, which concluded that stock options represented the best incentive for the top management to raise the overall value of the business and thus the oft-cited shareholder value. The Harvard study indicated that the best results were obtained by businesses that reward their management for increasing share value by means of share-related pay.

Executive share options are normally granted annually, and also sometimes at irregular intervals. This may depend on certain grant criteria: for example a minimum increase in turnover and/or profit over a period of some years before the options can be taken up.

Exercising the option is generally only permitted after a number of years (called the exercise period, or the vesting period; vesting means that the option can only be taken up after a specified period). Again, this can also be tied to conditions (exercise criteria): for example achieving a certain level in a peer group of businesses ('being among the first three or five of the most significant competitors'); or a rise in the share price of at least X. Such thresholds should create an additional incentive. Furthermore, profits should not appear to be earned too easily (windfall).

Sometimes it is also stipulated that the profit from options may only be realized in further shares, not in money. It may also be a condition of granting executive options that the beneficiary already owns a certain minimum number of company shares.

Share options that are still outstanding and have yet to be exercised will normally be forfeited if the holders leave the business of their own accord. On the other hand, when someone leaves with a 'golden handshake' the options can still be maintained by mutual agreement. Making the options dependent upon continued employment is some protection against other businesses wooing employees away. The effect is, however, limited. It very often happens that companies enticing employees away simply compensate them for the loss incurred by any forfeiture of options.

The valuation of executive share options warrants its own chapter. As already stated, there is no way to predict potential profit: it is not even certain that there will be a profit.

At least potentially, executive options can play a major role as part of the reward package, for very large sums indeed can be earned with these options. Because of this attempts have been made to make the unpredictable at least theoretically calculable and thereby reduce the wide-ranging and highly variable executive options to one common denominator so that they are open to comparison.

The most commonly recognized method for valuing options, futures and other derivatives in the financial markets is the formula developed by Black and Scholes. When the Black–Scholes model is applied to executive options, it should be adapted to take account of specific stipulations, such as the length of the exercise period. However, for 'usual' options, which are traded on the stock exchange, there are no such lengthy vesting periods or other restrictive conditions.

The Black–Scholes formula uses a number of variables in order to ascertain a *net present value* of executive options. The detailed formula itself need not be considered here. That can be left to specialists versed in mathematics. It is nevertheless interesting to see which are the most important variables and what influence they have on the valuation:

- *Share price:* A rise in the share price increases the value of the options.
- *Option price:* Reducing this price (setting the price at which the options can be exercised below the current rate when they were granted), increases the value of the option.
- *Risk-free rate of interest:* The rate of interest, for example, that is paid for government bonds; this gives the present value of the future expenses to be incurred when exercising the option; the higher the rate is, then the lower the cash value and also the greater the value of the option.
- *Duration of the option:* The longer the duration, the greater the value (a longer time span provides greater opportunity for the share price to rise).
- *Volatility of the share price:* The greater the volatility between upward and downward movement of share prices, then the greater the probability of gaining at some point a high profit from exercising the option. On the other hand, when the share price is stable over a long period, nothing is to be gained from the options.
- *Dividend yield:* The higher the yield, the lower the value of the option.

Alongside these rather complicated calculations there is yet another simple 'rule of thumb' method. Options awarded at irregular intervals or sizes are averaged out over the year. An estimate is made of how prices will develop until the end of the option period, either on the basis of past trends in price development or on the basis of the business objectives (possibly with a cautionary reduction). The difference between the current and the estimated price is the yield that can potentially be achieved at the end of the option period. This potential yield is discounted to its net present value, which then gives the income in relation to annual pay.

Should the gentle reader find this section on executive share options a little complicated and perhaps have to read it twice, then he or she is in good company. There are surprisingly many option holders who trustingly leave the 'technical details' to the experts.

For those who still want to know a little more about share options, then a series of alternatives that were mainly developed in the United States certainly provides interesting reading material. Not only are options the most widespread in the United States, but also the widest variety of methods are employed there, which with originality and innovation try to create increasingly effective incentives and rewards with increasingly new opportunities and risks.

- *Options for salary:* Share options replace pay rises. Hence there is a greater opportunity for profit for the manager (not forgetting the risk of loss, too, as the options can plunge 'under water'; see earlier); fixed salary costs are reduced.
- *Indexed options:* The price to be paid upon exercising the option is calculated according to the original rate at the time of the option being granted plus the increase in the relevant stock exchange index (Dow Jones, Nasdaq or particular industry indexes). Instead of an index the interest rate for risk-free investments (for instance government bonds) will sometimes also be taken into account. This should guarantee that a profit can only be made from the options when the rise in the share value is greater than the general trend.
- *Reload options:* As soon as the options are exercised new ones are awarded (of the same number of shares rather than the same value). The option price remains at the old rate and the exercise period remains the same as in the current plan. A common condition for *reloading* exercised options is that the shares must be kept. This has two purposes: on the one hand the options continue to exist despite being exercised; on the other hand, the obligation to retain the shares should both reinforce interest in their rising value and strengthen ties to the business.
- *Deposit share options:* The executives deposit the company shares they have, receiving in return a corresponding number of options. This should also broaden co-ownership and individual opportunities.
- *Premium options:* The option price is set higher than the actual rate when the options were awarded. This should guarantee that the option will only be exercised after a predetermined rise in price. Thus the shareholders are the first to profit from a price rise, then it is the turn of the people holding the options.
- *Purchased options:* The option holder pays about 10 per cent of the option value at the time it is granted. The exercise price will, however, be set at 90 per cent of the current rate at the time of the grant. Should the price fail to rise and the option not be exercised, then the deposit is forfeited: more incentive through greater risk.
- *Option performance vesting:* The share price must rise by a predetermined amount before the option can be exercised.
- *Exercise-hold incentives:* The holder of the option is given shares. There are restrictions on what the holder can do with these shares, for

they must be retained for a certain period. The number of shares granted in this way depends on the degree to which shares have been retained or not sold after exercising the option. Because this alternative concerns shares given away for free, there is considerable incentive to retain at least the profit gained after exercising the option in the form of shares. Once again the idea is to augment the executives' interest in the rising value of the business while they increase their own personal holding of shares.

And Without Shares?

Not all businesses are joint-stock companies and not all joint-stock organizations are listed on the stock exchange. Where there are no shares, there can be no share options.

There is, however, a scheme known as *phantom shareholding*. The value of each business can of course be determined: this value allows a share simulation to be derived. When from time to time (or even regularly) the value of a business is determined anew, a fictional development in the share price can be contrived.

This process is not entirely easy and the results do not have the objectivity and authority that is peculiar to the real stock exchange. On the other hand the phantom values are less (or even not at all) subject to the arbitrary influences that often affect the stock exchange, where rises or falls in shares sometimes seem to have little to do with actual events in the business concerned (though in the longer term the value of the business and the share price mostly run smoothly alongside one another).

It is possible to form share option plans on the basis of phantom shares. These will not be 'the real thing' however. It should be remembered that from the point of view of costs, profits from phantom shares must be paid out of the business's own coffers. In the case of real options they come from the share market (at least if the business has purchased its own shares for coverage at the time of granting the options; see above).

When there are no shares and the creation of phantom shares does not seem appropriate, that can still be compensated for by placing greater emphasis on the business's own long-term incentive (bonus) plans.

CHAPTER 8

Conclusion

- We have seen what *motivation* is and know how vital it is as a basis of achievement-oriented activity.
- *Performance* is the fulfilment of certain tasks within the context of the business. Its quality and quantity is measured and evaluated according to the criteria of the task and the objectives. This evaluation is at the same time a mechanism for constructive feedback.
- *Performance potential* is what a person contributes to their future development, which can then in turn be encouraged by the business.
- The widely varied forms of *reward* represent what the business gives to its employees in return for all of the above. At the same time reward is also a fair market value.
- *Incentives* or *incentive systems* are a special form of reward. They place the focus of performance on very concrete objectives and at the same time reward the achievement of these objectives.

Motivation, performance, feedback, incentive, reward: all are closely interrelated. They are essentially unaffected by faddish modifications. It is only in the ways they are described, how they are incorporated into systems and guided and applied in practice, that they are subject to cultural influences and to the effects of permanently changing economic and social conditions.

There has been in this book an attempt to follow the principle that was outlined in the introduction. When it comes to understanding principles and fundamental preconditions, for example with motivation and how it differs from incentive, or the essence of potential and how it differs from performance, then it is worthwhile to tap into the widest possible variety of sources that can help to generate understanding. But as far as the application of certain systems and techniques are concerned, then mechanisms are at play that should be as simple as possible: only as complex as is absolutely necessary for their ability to function.

It is not likely that the fundamental significance of motivation, performance, potential and reward will, in comparison to the past or present, change considerably in the future. It will certainly not decrease. On the contrary, the importance of these factors and even more so their essence, which only people can offer, will probably increase. The capacity and desire to perform, development potential, the ability and willingness to learn, talent, knowledge and creativity are qualities that only people can furnish and that cannot be cultivated at will. On the contrary, they seem to be becoming more and more scarce. Indeed, the opportunities for development, education and training seem to be lagging both quantitatively and qualitatively behind the relentless growth in the earth's population.

Regional differences are known to be enormous. It might be assumed that 'rich' Europe, which economically, socially and culturally can look back on a long development and a great tradition, is in a favourable situation. However, this does not seem to be true. The statistics are alarming:

In 1960 the average age for Europeans was 32 years, in 1995 it was 36 and in 2025 it will be 45.

In 2025 there will allegedly be 50 per cent more pensioners than there are today. The age statistic is unquestionably correct, because it is a simple calculation with few variables. The prediction for the number of pensioners is a different matter altogether. It can only be reasonable accurate if the retirement age remains the same. However, that will certainly not be the case. It will change, not only because it must, but because it has always changed.

Age is therefore not the problem. The really important, interesting and ultimately decisive question is how it will affect motivation, the ability and willingness to perform, training and development. That is not only a question for the politicians or for the schools and universities, nor only for businesses or for people, who have to get their bearings. It represents a crucial question and an essential undertaking for everyone involved.

There is also talk of X millions (three, four, five?) of people being needed in Europe to balance out the shortfall in the work force: not by 2025 but already in 2002 or 2003. Even if these gaps, however large they may really be, are to be plugged by tremendously effective training schemes, by activating reserves of the work force (women? the elderly?) or by immigration from other countries (which ones?), it again qualitatively centres around the same question: of motivation, performance, potential, ability, experience and talent.

Perhaps – hopefully – this book can contribute to discovering the answers to these questions. One thing is certain: those with the best answers will be one step ahead. That has always been true, although now it is becoming more critical: in a world where borders governing geography and time are coming down, advantages will be increasingly decisive and disadvantages increasingly ruinous.

BIBLIOGRAPHY

Argyris, C. (1960). *Personality and Organization*. New York: Wiley.

Chen, C. C. Ford, C. M. and Farris, G. F. (1999). Do Rewards Benefit the Organization? *IEEE Transactions on Engineering Management*, Vol. 46, No.1. New York: IEEE Engineering Management Society.

Duden. (1963). *Das Herkunftswörterbuch. Eine Etymologie der deutschen Sprache*. Mannheim/Vienna/Zurich.

Festinger, L. (1977). *Theory of Cognitice Dissonance*. Evanston.

Hall, W. (1995). *Managing Cultures: Making Strategic Relations Work*. Chichester, UK: Wiley.

Herzberg, F. W., Mausner, B. and Snyderman, B. (1959). *The Motivation to Work*. New York.

Hofstede, G. (1991). *Cultures and Organisation, Software of the Mind*. London: McGraw Hill.

Hofstede, G. (1994). *Allemaal Andersdenkenden, Omgaan met cultuurverschillen*. Amsterdam: Uiteverij Contact.

Kohn, A. (1993). *Punished by Rewards*. New York, Boston: Houghton Mifflin.

Kressler, H. W. (1989). *Leistungsbeurteilung von Managern* (Evaluating Managers' Performance). Vienna: Wirtschaftsverlag Carl Ueberreuter.

Kressler, H. W. (1993). *Personalmanagement im neuen Europa* (Personnel Management in the New Europe). Vienna: Wirtschaftsverlag Carl Ueberreuter.

Leavitt, H. J., Pondy, L. and Boje, D. M. (eds) (1980). *Readings in Managerial Psychology*. Chicago, London: University of Chicago Press.

Locke, E. A. (1968). Toward a Theory of Task Motivation. *Organizational Behavior and Human Performance*, No. 3.

Locke, E. A. and Latham, G. P. (1992). *Theory of Goal Setting and Task Performance*. New Jersey: Prentice Hall.

Lueger, G. (1993). *Die Bedeutung der Wahrnehmung bei der Personalbeurteilung*. Munich, Mering: Rainer Hampp Verlag.

Maslow, A. H. (1954). *A Theory of Human Motivation*. New York: Harper and Row.

McClelland, D. C. (1961). *The Achieving Society.* Princeton, New Jersey.

McClelland, D. C., Spencer Jr., L. M. and Spencer, S. M. (1992). *Competency Assessment Methods.* Hay/McBär Research Press.

McGregor, D. (1960). *The Human Side of Enterprise.* New York: McGraw Hill.

Mitrani, A., Dalziel, M. and Fitt, D. (eds) (1992). *Competency Based Human Resource Management.* London: Kogan Page.

Musil, R. (1952). *Der Mann ohne Eigenschaften* (Man Without Characteristics). Hamburg: Rowohlt.

Peters, T. J., and Waterman Jr., R. H. (1982). *In Search of Excellence.* New York: Harper and Row.

Reiss, S. (2000). *Who am I? The Sixteen Basic Desires that Motivate our Behavior and Define our Personality.* New York: Jeremy P. Tarcher/Putnam.

Staehle, W. H. (1991). *Management.* Munich: Verlag Franz Vahlen.

Taylor, F. W. (1911). *Principles of Scientific Management.* New York.

Vroom, V. H. (1964). *Work and Motivation.* New York: Wiley.

Weinert, A. B. (1998). *Organisationspsychologie.* Weinheim: Psychologie Verlags Union.